In The Driving Seat

In The Driving Seat

ALEX HEYMER

Old Pond Publishing

First published 2009

ISBN: 978-1-905523-96-2

A catalogue record for this book is available from the
British Library

Published by
Old Pond Publishing Ltd
Dencora Business Centre
36 Whitehouse Road
Ipswich
IP1 5LT
United Kingdom

www.oldpond.com

Cover design by Liz Whatling
Typesetting by Galleon Typesetting, Ipswich
Printed and bound in Malta by Gutenberg Press

Contents

Dedication

To Janne
who thought I had left home while I was
writing my memoirs
and to my daughters Angela and Lee-Anne

Introduction

IN my younger years, motor vehicles were the 'in thing' as there weren't many about. Horses were still the order of transport and not many people, my father included, could afford a car. I do remember my friend Ron's father owning an Austin 7 Ruby saloon; I thought he must have been rich.

So to be able to drive a mechanical machine was like being a hero and to be able to drive a lorry was like being a superhero. This is what I thought of my father and I wanted to be just like him.

Lorries were very basic when I started, with no power steering, air-assisted clutches, air braking, cab heating or air conditioning. I even remember my father using bike clips on his trousers because of the draught from the foot pedal holes. Changing gear was like stopping; you had to double the clutch movement to slow the clutch plate and wait for the revs to drop before you could select your next gear. The Bedfords I first worked on were still rod and cable braking.

Synchromesh and automatic gear boxes then came into being and now vehicles are so improved that most people have a car, women are driving trucks and buses and the roads are much more congested. I often wonder what my father would have thought of modern trucks. Today, driving is a matter of everyday life and is of no major significance.

I had never intended to write a manuscript about my driving years. I was quite happy in my retirement, enjoying many things such as crosswords and reading, and Janne gets me doing the odd job around the house to help with the decorating.

However, I still get the newsletters from my old employer, Tankfreight Tanker Division (now Excel) every so often, and in one of these I saw that a driver had written of his driving career and experiences on general haulage. After reading this book I began searching for more, and it then occurred to me that I had a few stories to tell myself, some serious and some funny; 'I could do that', I decided. I hadn't thought that a lorry driver's account of life on the road would appeal to anyone except perhaps another driver, but I had found this one very interesting, so I sat down and started to recall my life as I saw it.

Once I'd started I think Janne felt as if I'd left home, because I would spend all day on the computer with my memoirs. Well, it kept me quiet. Obviously this book is a shortened version of things, as some were unprintable, but I found the main theme, once again following in my father's footsteps: lorry driving.

Chapter 1

Early Days

I was born in December 1932 in an upstairs flat of a house in Helena Road, Plaistow, East London. When my mother saw me, she exclaimed, 'Oh no, not a ginger baby!' The midwife was kinder, saying that many women of the day would give anything for that colour hair.

My parents were born and brought up in Bow, East London, and made the move to Plaistow just before my birth. My father, a lorry driver, drove for Bouts Tillotson, a major haulage company of the day. As soon as I was old enough to understand, I wanted to be like him, and it took all my mother's time and patience to look after me while I played lorry drivers.

I used to watch my father going to work in his big overcoat and flat cap and pleaded with my mother to get me the same outfit. Although she tried, she couldn't find one, until she happened to mention it to the lady in the downstairs flat. 'I have a coat that's too small for my son. Do you want it?' she replied.

My mother wrapped the coat up, so when I unwrapped it, as far as I was concerned it was brand new. I also had a cap to go with it. I used to take ages putting this coat on, hunching my shoulders and jumping up and down to get the coat to reach my neck. Then I would put on my cap. I had seen my father do this many times.

I had a small pedal car too. I would knock on our kitchen door and when my mother opened it she would say, 'Hello, Al. Come home for a cuppa?'

'Is it all right to bring my driver's mate in?' I would ask.

'Sure,' she would reply, making me a cup of tea.

My mother has told me that I would take off my hat and coat. Then, when I decided I was leaving, I would spend ages going through the whole routine of putting them back on again. On top of that there were the noises I made of lorry engines. I used to drive her mad, she said.

One time I kept whining with a bad earache. My father went out and bought me a big box lorry which I could sit on and push with my feet. On the side in big letters was *Bouts Tillotson Ltd.* I soon stopped crying.

We had a wooden table with a small drop-down flap. My mother told me that I used to play for ages putting this flap up and down and making out it was my tail board.

I used to listen to my father telling my mother stories of what had happened at work, including the practical jokes. One involved a young boy who had started but could not read or write and seemed a little backward. None of the other drivers had wanted the boy, so my father offered to take him, and every spare moment they had my father would teach him to read and write.

They used to have to go to a central distribution centre where all the haulage contractors assembled to be given loads, and while they waited in the outside office they would kick a football about. One day my father told the office clerk to call the boy over in the morning when he came in. The clerk was to tell the boy that while they were playing with the ball the bouncing and vibration had broken the office clock (apparently it was an old station clock). The boy looked devastated at the news. He did not earn enough to pay for the repairs.

'What's wrong?' my father asked.

The boy explained the situation. My father said, 'Well, get it mended and the drivers will have a collection to pay for it.'

When my father called in at the boy's house to have a cup of tea, the boy's mother said, 'Please thank the drivers for what they have done. They must think a lot of him to do that.'

My father came out red-faced. 'Serves you right!' said my mother.

The boy's family were all dockers and eventually the boy followed his brothers and father into the docks, but they never forgot what my father had done for him. They became great friends with my parents and we often visited them in Custom House.

My parents were a lively pair. I remember one time my father started laughing when he came home for a cuppa and saw that my mother had made a jam tart.

'What are you laughing at?' my mother asked.

'We were in the café, and one of the drivers bought tea and jam tarts. When his boy came in he smacked the jam tarts in the boy's face.'

'That's not nice,' my mother said, but before anything else could happen my father had smacked the jam tart in *her* face. So it was no jam tarts today!

My mother was always cooking cakes and scones. One day when my father called in for a cuppa my mother had made a mince tart. As she came into the living room she dropped it. My father was quite upset.

'I've a good mind to throw it at you,' he said. So she dared him and the battle started, all in good fun.

My mother later said that she found mince pie for ages after when she was cleaning.

My father left Bouts, and got a job with more money, driving for Towler and Sons boilermakers. This suited me fine, because then he could take my mother and me out in his lorry, an International.

Whenever my father took us out I insisted we stopped at a transport café. I would keep running to the door to make sure the lorry was all right. 'Come and sit down,' my father would say. 'Nobody's going to take it.'

We moved to a downstairs flat in Stratford soon after this. My mother took me shopping in the local area and on the way back we came down the next road to ours where I saw a small café, no more than five hundred yards from our house. I couldn't wait to tell my father about my find: 'Dad, instead of coming in for a cuppa we can go round to the café!' I could just imagine what he thought.

I was five years old and getting ready to start school when my mother told me I was going to have a baby brother or sister. 'You'll have to save up all your farthings,' she said. The baby turned out to be a sister named Catherine.

I started at school just before the war began, in January 1938. My father was exempt from the forces as Towler and Sons were making munitions such as invasion barges.

We stayed in London, but when my parents thought it was getting too bad my uncle came round in one of his firm's vans and picked us all up and took us out into the country. There were three families: my mother and her two sisters, with seven children altogether.

I don't know where we were meant to go, but we finished up in Dane End, Hertfordshire. We just happened to stop outside the cottage in which the village school headmaster lived. When we children heard the words 'school' and 'teacher' we all ducked down out of sight.

The headmaster arranged for the villagers to assemble in the village hall, where we were all allocated to lodge with one of the villagers. My mother, sister and I were billeted on Lordship farm.

I was the only male amongst nine females and in the evenings we all congregated together. They taught me to knit and do embroidery. When I embroidered two chair-back covers and gave them to the farmer's wife she said, 'When I look at them I will think of the little evacuee boy who stayed with us.'

We shared a large bedroom with a big bay window around which was a window box. I used to sit on the box and look out the side window – my windscreen – and drive my mother mad with my engine noises, including the pre-selected gearboxes on the buses, although at that time I didn't know what type of gearbox it was.

Friday was shopping day in the town of Hertford. We would walk into the village and get the Green Line bus into town. The bus was a half-cab coach, and I could not take my eyes off the driver, with his overcoat collar up round his neck (there were no heaters then).

Also staying at the farm was a London teacher whose husband was a London fireman, later killed in the bombing. I couldn't read or write, so in the evenings she would teach me.

I had not yet used pen and ink. On my first day at the village school I made a big blot on my exercise book. I thought I would be clever by scratching it out with my pen. I dried my pen and started scratching. I thought I had made a good job, only to find I had a hole right through the book.

The teacher was not impressed with this and gave me a good caning. When I got back to the farm and told my mother she went mad. First thing in the morning she waited for the teacher and in no uncertain terms told him that if he ever touched me again his feet would not touch the ground!

I was envious of the village boys because they wore riding britches and had nice bicycles with pump-up tyres. If they had a puncture they went to the village blacksmith.

My father managed to get down most weekends and one weekend he came with a nice blue bicycle. I could not wait to get a puncture so I could go to the blacksmith's forge.

A steep hill ran from the village school to the farm. My friend had an old-fashioned ladies' bike and I was chasing him down the hill when he fell off. I could not stop and went straight into him. I picked myself up, battered and bruised, but could not believe my eyes: my bike had disintegrated into parts that were all over the place. I could not manage to carry all the bits under my arms; in my hands I was trying to manage the wheels, frame, forks and pedals. It was a total disaster. I found out that my dad had bought the bike from a junk shop. It was scrap.

We used to help out on the farm which was owned by two brothers, one of whom had a false leg following a motorbike accident. This brother looked after the poultry, making his way across the field with a bucket of chicken food and whistling as he threw the feed out. It was quite a sight to see the chickens and turkeys spread out across the field.

The farmer asked me if I would like to do the feeding. With my bucket of feed I would copy him by whistling and throwing the feed to the ground, quite proud that they did not notice the difference between me and the farmer. However, one of the turkeys would always make a bee-line for me, half-flying across and trying to peck my legs. All I could do was hold the bucket in front of me and try to ward him off.

One weekend my father said, 'I'll come with you.'

'Here he comes,' I said when we got into the field. My father took fright.

When we told my mother, she said, 'Next time take a big stick and hit him with it.'

That's what I did. I gave the bird such a whack over the head that I saw his eyes roll. He staggered away never to bother me again.

I also used to fetch the cows in for milking. Wearing my welly boots and slapping them with my stick I was quite proud as I ushered the herd in. The cows knew when it was milking time and stood by the gate ready. Although most of them went to their own places in the stalls in the shed, a few were crafty and nicked food from someone else's stall until they were ushered out.

One of the cowmen while milking once asked my sister if she had seen the bottom of the cow's teat. 'No,' she said, and bent down to look. The cowman gave the teat a squirt into her face and we all laughed.

While we were at the farm we would hear the German bombers going into London and back again. One night we were sitting taking it easy when there was an almighty WHOOSH! We fell out of our chairs on to the floor. The next morning the farmer found a parachute in the fields. He alerted the police and army thinking a German had landed, but it turned out to be a land mine that had buried itself in the soft earth.

We were told that some of the bombers would unload

their bombs rather than going into London so that they could make a quick exit home. When the bomb disposal squad came we were evacuated for the day to Hertford where we heard the bomb go off.

For a short period we came home to London, sleeping at night in the garden shelter. During this time I became dangerously ill with pneumonia and pleurisy and I was not expected to live. I was rushed into Whipps Cross hospital and was so ill that they could not put me to sleep to operate and I had to have the operation while I was conscious. They froze my back and the surgeons got me to hold their hands while the operation took place. 'If it hurts, squeeze our hands,' they said, and afterwards: 'What a good boy!' One of the surgeons gave me five shillings, and the other gave me ten shillings.

While I was in the hospital a man in the next bed told me he was a lorry driver and he had knocked his knee up getting on the back of his lorry. It looked really painful. We talked about driving and I got to really enjoy our chats. He had numerous operations but eventually they had to amputate his leg as they could do no more for him.

A couple of days later I found his bed empty when I woke in the morning. 'Has he gone home?' I asked the nurse.

'No,' she replied. 'He died in the night.' I was shocked. I couldn't believe that he had died and I had slept through it all.

I was in hospital for six months. They placed a rubber tube in my back to drain the fluid from my lungs into a bottle under the bed. For Christmas 1943 the nurses gave me a book as a Christmas present. I was eleven years old.

When I left hospital we stayed for about six months in

Glasgow with friends of my mother. Then we returned home.

I remember once playing with a bat and ball outside the house while my sister was crying from wanting the bat. I would not let her have it, so my father came out and said, 'If you keep arguing, no one will have it,' and took the bat indoors.

Our front door had a glass panel that rattled, and I thought to myself, I will aim the ball at the door and the glass will rattle and frighten my father. I took careful aim and threw the ball and it went straight through the window, into the hallway. I did not know whether to run or face my father.

He told me afterwards that he could not stop laughing and had thought I was saying, 'You took the bat, now you can have the ball.' He said the glass wanted replacing anyway.

I had a three-wheel bike and as I rode by a house up the street the girl who lived there would always punch me in the back and I kept coming home crying. Eventually my father said, 'Give me that bike,' and he threw it up the garden, buckling one of the rear wheels, so that when I rode it my bum used to wobble.

As the war came to an end my father applied to London Transport and he started on the trams. I used to watch him getting dressed in the clothes he put on to drive the tram; they did not have windscreens so he had a coat over another coat, and then a big rain mac, goggles, and a bus man's hat with the strap under his chin. One day my aunt came round and they dressed her in my father's clothes – she could not stand up with the weight of them.

The progression from trams to trolleybuses took place around this time. My friend (whose father was also a bus driver) and I used to get the sixpenny all-day and meet up with our fathers to ride on their buses, because they were on different routes.

After a few years on the buses, my father returned to Towler and Sons and lorry driving. I remember on one of my trips with him he ran over a bird and I would not talk to him, calling him a murderer. He soon pulled up and went back, telling me that the bird was all right and had flown away, but I knew he was only saying that because I was upset.

I couldn't wait to go out in the lorry with my father and get on the back to help unloading. One day when we did a delivery the man gave me sixpence. I told my father that the man had given me some money, and he said, 'That's your beer money.' I asked him what beer money was, and he replied that it was for helping the man.

We did the same delivery another time and I remembered this man and my beer money, but when we started to leave I said to my father 'That man forgot my beer money!' My father then got out and went round the back of the lorry, getting sixpence out of his pocket and told me the man had forgotten and had apologised (he told me the whole story later).

A good friend and I went out in the lorry one time for a ride. My friend wanted to ride on the back, but my father refused, saying, 'It's too cold,' but my friend kept on at him, so my father did put us on the back and after a couple of miles going round roundabouts my friend was sick, so we got back into the cab.

We went out in the lorry another time and were on the back trying to help in our own way, when my father said to the man unloading, 'Make out that they have caught your hand'. The next thing I knew, this man was hopping about holding his hand and shouting that we had hurt it; so then we were very reluctant to get on the back and help again, until my father told us he was only kidding.

My father came home one day and said to me, 'How would you like to go on a journey?' I asked where to, and he replied, 'Stafford. I have to get some machinery and we will be out two nights.' My mother was worried for me but my father said I would be all right. I could not wait. My first taste of distance work and lodging; I could not be happier.

My father was always noted for his joking. Once, in the London docks waiting for a load with a few drivers having a smoke, he was in the brown suit that he had been given, with bicycle clips to stop the draft coming up through the pedals.

Some PLA (Port of London Authority) officials came along and called my father over to speak to him. When he returned, the other drivers asked what they had wanted with him. My father replied that the men were going to move the barges and bring them back for him in the morning and had asked him if that would be all right, so my father had said 'yes'. The drivers started laughing because the PLA men had thought he was the dock ganger.

Another time when he was waiting, two drivers approached him and asked, 'Excuse us, mate, but will we be unloaded today?'

My father replied, 'Are you heavy or light lift?'

They said, 'Heavy. Only you sent us away yesterday and told us to come back today.'

My father said, 'No, it wasn't me.' They both insisted it was him, until he said, 'That's my lorry there and I'm waiting as well.'

They were full of apologies, saying, 'We were sure it was you.'

I attended Whitehall Modern Secondary School, which was at the end of Forest Lane, opposite Forest Gate station. I became a prefect and enjoyed my remaining school years.

I remember in particular one funny thing that happened at school. My friends and I used to visit a local café. One evening we left the café in the dark and got on our bikes to ride home, giving our mates who did not have bikes a 'crossbar' ride, even though we had no lights.

Suddenly a policeman came out of the shadows pushing his bike and stopped us. He made us give our names and addresses, some gave false names of course, and then he made us turn our bikes upside down to get the serial numbers. Eventually he got to his bike, standing on the kerb, and wanted to know whose bike it was. He had a huge rant at us for not owning up to whose bike it was, and proceeded to turn it upside down to get the serial number, and then realised it was his own. I think he was quite embarrassed and told us to clear off and he would be looking out for us in future. We could just not stop laughing; we all thought 'What a nutter.'

I remember as well being taken to my first football match at West Ham by my father when I was about six years old. We stood on the terraces, freezing cold, and I was cuffing my runny nose on my coat sleeve, not a bit interested in watching the football. In any case, I could not see over the people in front of me, and this made sure I was never a football supporter.

Sixty-seven years later I returned, after an invitation from my thirteen-year-old grandson, both daughters and my son in law, and was now able to sit down, so I really enjoyed it.

My school days were coming to an end, and I had one thing on my mind – driving. Both my father and uncle tried talking me out of it. My uncle told me there was no money in driving and that electricity was the thing of today, so why didn't I take that up as a career.

However, I could not be told, my mind was made up, so my father said, 'Well, if that's the case, why don't you get a job in a garage, and find out all you can about motors. Then, when you're old enough, see how you feel.' I still had four years before I could drive anyway, so my father talked me into going into a garage rather than being a van boy.

When my father took me out in the lorry he used to let me have a go. I was twelve years old but looked older than my age and my father would say, 'Sit in the corner of the seat and rest your elbow on the door, so if anybody sees us they will think you are a real driver.'

I used to make a right hash of the gear changing and when I let the clutch up I nearly broke both the half-shafts (I think it was because I could hardly reach the pedals). About this time, a man who my father knew bought a Hillman Minx car, and asked my father if he would teach him to drive. My father agreed, so in the evenings when the man went home, my father and I would take the car back to the garage and my father would let me have a go at driving that. I kept driving on the right side of the road, which always made my father say, 'We are not on the Continent yet!' I was starting to get very depressed about my driving skills.

But at the age of fourteen I left school to make my mark on the motor and transport industry.

Chapter 2

Starting Out

TO get me started, my father took me to a small garage in Leytonstone High Road. The manager there explained that I could have an apprenticeship if I wanted.

'I've got a boy here who, if asked, could tell you how many grease nipples there are on any make of car you care to mention,' he said.

This turned out to be true, but as far as the apprenticeship went, I think this was a red herring. He promised that I would be sent to all the car manufacturers during my apprenticeship for trade training, but I wasn't there long enough to find out.

Some of the fitters fascinated me. One was an ex-navy man who, no matter what job he did, would walk out at the end of the day as clean as he had started in the morning. Another was a middle-aged man who could not drive a car. I could not believe that he could pull a car to pieces, without being able to drive it. They had another younger fitter who wore an old army overcoat, and I thought to myself, 'I must get one of those.' He did look out of the ordinary.

There were a couple of boys at the garage and, being the more junior, I was puncture boy. However, one day the manager asked me, 'Will you wash the governor's car?' I had never washed a car before, so I got a bucket of water and a piece of rag and basically just moved all the mud and dirt around the car so that it looked worse than it had before I started! The manager came out and nearly had a fit. He rushed into the garage to get one of the other boys to help me before the governor saw it and had a fit himself.

Another time, an elderly fitter was building up an engine he was reconditioning. He had the engine, minus the cylinder head, on a trestle, when he decided to go for a haircut.

Having just repaired a puncture, I came into the garage and took two half crowns out of my pocket. I approached one of the boys who happened to be standing by the engine, and boasted, 'Look, beer money!' With that he hit my hand, sending the coins spinning in the air so that they dropped straight into the push-rod apertures of the engine.

There was panic on both our faces as we ran to the other fitters and explained what had happened. They came over, picked the engine up and turned it over, shaking it like a money box until the two coins fell out. I was so relieved as I had had visions of the fitter having to strip the engine down again. When he came back we all simply remarked what a nice haircut he had had. If only he knew!

On the corner of Sugar House Lane and the main Stratford to Bow Road was Jessups, the main Vauxhall and Bedford distributors, very close to Towler and Sons where my father still was, which was at the end of the cul-de-sac. My father spoke to the foreman at Jessups and I went there for an interview. I was promised an apprenticeship when I was sixteen years old. I had been at Leytonstone garage about six months by this time.

I started on a Monday morning; I was issued with a boiler suit and introduced to the fitter I would be working with, called Harry. I was excited to learn that we were going to do an engine change on an ex-army Bedford lorry; I had not done anything so technical before. We got started, Harry telling me all the nuts and bolts I had to remove from the front grill, and which spanners from his tool box I would need.

The first nut and bolt I began to undo was so rusty and corroded that it broke. I was devastated and had to go and find Harry who was waiting at the stores for some parts. I explained what had happened. 'Will I have to tell the foreman?' I asked, worried that he would sack me.

But Harry replied, 'Don't worry, they will all be replaced anyway, and you'll find that most of them will break.' I then explained that at the Leytonstone garage there was a court of enquiry if you broke a nut and bolt, because money saved was money gained.

From then on I began to settle down and took every opportunity to get behind the wheel (the slang for this was 'clutch-happy').

Opposite the garage was a pub, and behind the pub was a piece of waste ground, possibly bomb damaged, where Jessups put all their road-worthy vehicles, and did small repairs.

One of the boys was told to show me how to clean spark plugs. He demonstrated how to sand blast them, gap them and then test them, but the plug we were testing did not spark. 'Perhaps the wire is not on properly,' I said, and went to take the wire off. I got a big electric shock.

He shouted at me, 'What are you doing? You bloody fool!'

I shouted back, 'I thought you had taken your finger off the button!'

The man who did all the grease and oil changes used to put engine oil on his hair, insisting that it made his hair grow thicker; it was just a shame it did nothing for his brain.

Me and some of the boys used to get in early, pull the shutters up and drive the non-essential vehicles over the road onto the waste ground. I would also always be on standby with a car, lorry or van to take my father down to his firm at the bottom of Sugar House Lane when he got off the bus, trying to impress him with my driving.

One time I took him down the lane in a small 'artic', and by the time he had watched me turn it around I think he was late for work, but he always encouraged me in my driving.

One evening Harry told me that the ex-army lorry on the front had no brakes, and the servo and master cylinder had not been put back on yet, so I should take it carefully in the morning.

I arrived early and got the shutters up pronto. I jumped into the lorry, and all over the cab in chalk was 'NO BRAKES'. I thought to myself, 'I know, I don't have to be told again,' so I started it up and drove steadily out of the garage, thinking I would try a bit of gear changing. I got up to second gear and turned right to go into the bomb site. Those lorries did not have much steering lock so I realised I was going to hit the brick wall. I went for the brakes and . . . nothing happened. I hit the wall and knocked part of it down, as well as damaging the lorry.

I had to go and see the manager and he gave me a right rollicking, saying, 'I know you boys come in early and practise your driving skills, but be more bloody careful in future.'

Another time Harry told me to get a car from the bomb site to work on. As I pulled up I ran the handbrake up the ratchet, just as the manager was walking by. He stopped and stared at me. 'Do not ever let me see or hear you do that again,' he said. 'Push the button in and lift it, a good driver never runs it up the ratchet like that.' Another lesson was learnt.

One of our fitters had an artificial leg. Once he was lying under a car just inside the garage entrance, with all four wheels off and the car on stands. Just as he got out and went to his bench one of the boys came flying in and hit the car, knocking it to the ground. There was a loud crash and every one rushed to the garage entrance to see what had happened. The fitter who had been working on it saw the car on the ground which he should have been under and fainted.

I also remember an accident happening when two boys took a lorry down Sugar House Lane. One stood at the back of the lorry watching the other reversing, with his arm up, beckoning as they were getting close to a wall. However, he managed to get his arm wedged between the lorry and the wall and broke it.

I was the garage tea boy, so it was my responsibility to get all the mugs out and put them on the fire stove in the engine room (where the engines were reconditioned). One day the manager came in and as he walked past he stopped, looked at the mugs, and suddenly threw the lot in the dustbin. 'Go and see the foreman, get some petty cash and buy some new ones,' he said to me, 'Don't use cracked mugs.'

I had been at Jessups for six months when Harry asked me if I had had my beer money yet (it was coming up to Christmas). I suspiciously replied that I hadn't, so he said, 'Well, see Alf the foreman and ask him for it.' I was reluctant, thinking that this just had to be a windup.

We both approached the foreman and Harry simply

said, 'Al wants his beer money.' I half-expected Alf to say, 'Piss off,' but he got his notebook out of his top pocket saying, 'You have £18 to come,' and wadded me out with some cash. Considering my pay was about £4 10s a week, I was rich! Apparently the scrap metal and customer tips were all handed to the foreman to be shared evenly amongst the boys.

One of the fitters was called Chipperfield, Chippy for short. He dealt with all the breakdowns so I asked if I could be his mate for a while. Harry was a bit upset but admitted that it would be good experience for me, so I was to be the new boy on breakdowns. I could not wait to be called out, anything to be on the road. The only snag was that Chippy was a chain smoker. He would have a cigarette in his mouth that he wouldn't touch until it was about to burn his lip. He would then take out another from the packet and put it in the other side of his mouth, taking the smaller one out and lighting the new one. This carried on all day. It would get to the stage when I would look across to him and think, 'Why don't you get another out of the packet?'

All the boys at the garage smoked, so I soon followed suit. Chippy looked at me one day and said, 'Let me see you smoke that cigarette.' I looked at him, inhaled and puffed out, and he exclaimed, 'Oh! So you don't take it down.' I asked him what he meant, and he replied, 'Take a big draw in and swallow it.' I did as he said, and coughed my heart out; I had soon thrown all my cigarettes away and have never smoked since. I thanked him for that – but it was too late for him to stop.

The breakdown wrecker was a short wheelbase Bedford (most likely a Tipper Chassis). Sometimes when we had to lift a very heavy vehicle with its crane, the front of the wrecker would come off the ground and, as we had no steering, we had to carry sand bags to keep the front wheels down.

During our tea breaks we all sat round the fire stove eating our sandwiches and drinking our tea. For entertainment one of the boys brought a shock machine in; we would hold hands and sit there shaking with the electric shock.

I always remember a good-looking sixteen-year-old who worked there called Alfie. During our tea breaks he used to tell us about his girlfriend, always mentioning her silk underwear. We all sat glued to our chairs with eyes like organ stops. I think he took great delight in seeing the expressions on our faces.

Women were always the subject of conversation, we were even told about the 'ladies of the night'. I often could not believe what I was hearing.

One evening a friend and I started to discuss what we had heard about all of this, so we decided to try it out. We took the underground to Soho and walked along Wardour Street to see these ladies standing in doorways, but nothing happened. My friend then decided to walk on the other side of the road to see if this would help. Very quickly a lady approached me, saying something in my ear, but I only caught the word 'time'; so I looked at my watch and said, 'Nine-thirty' and hurried on. My friend rushed over to find out what she'd said. When I told him he fell about laughing and said, 'She was asking you if you wanted a short time!' Then I started laughing and he said, 'Come on, let's go home. We've proved them right.' So we headed home a little wiser.

Once when we were on a breakdown, Chippy wanted some cigarettes, so we stopped for him to run into a newsagent's. They only had cork-tipped ones which he didn't like, but he lit up anyway. Later I looked over to him and noticed his trousers were smouldering. I shouted to him, 'Your trousers are alight!' He looked down and tried to damp it out with his hand. I then looked back up and realised that the traffic had stopped, but by the time I could warn him we had hit the car in front. It turned out that while he still had the cork tip in his mouth, the end of the cigarette had dropped off. 'That's why I hate those bloody cigarettes,' he grumbled.

On a breakdown in High Street, East Ham, we arrived to find that a furniture lorry had broken down. The lorry was petrol, as most vehicles at the time were, and a forward control with the engine in the cab, so we had the cowling up and were checking the ignition for spark, with our heads directly over the engine, when Chippy took the distributor cap off and flicked the points which were sparking. He put the distributor rotor arm in the cap on the plug lead segment and by sheer chance it was the next cylinder to fire. As he flicked the points there was an enormous 'bang'. We both jumped out of our skins, thinking the lorry had blown up. Ever since then I have always been wary when checking the ignition systems, and stand well back.

Chippy was partly deaf. This proved to be a problem when we had to get a furniture van out from a yard on one occasion. We hooked a rope onto the vehicle and began to move out of the yard, him driving out with the wrecker and me in tow. It was tight; I could see that we were not going to make it, so I started to blow the hooter frantically, but he did not hear me. The back end of the body struck the wall pillar and tore a gouge from the van.

He got out and said, 'Well, that came out all right, didn't it?'

I looked at him and said, 'No, not really, look at the body!'

'What!' he replied. 'Have we done that?'

Once when Chippy was off sick, the foreman said to me, 'You know where Chippy lives. Can you go round his house and get the trade plates which he took home?' So I got on my bike and rode round to his house. I knocked on the door and leant my hand on it. Two men in white overalls approached and stood looking at me. One of the men said, 'Are you quite comfortable there?'

I thought, 'What is he on about?'

'Take your hand off the door,' he said. I peeled my hand off, and there was my palm print in the freshly grained (but not painted) door; they were really not amused. I could just imagine them saying, 'Look at that prat.'

It was not all work and no play. We would often wind the older fitters up to get our own back for the strokes they pulled on us. One trick was to connect the plug tester on the metal tops of the work benches. When the fitter came to the bench to put the parts in the paraffin tray, we would quickly push the button and send a shock wave down the bench, watching him jump. We had to quickly run and hide before he could find out who had done it.

The fitters were once larking about with a boy and went as far as to strip off his trousers and pants, tying him to the stanchion. They then put axle grease on his private parts. When the manager happened to walk by the boy exclaimed, 'Look what they have done to me sir!'

The manager just said, 'Serves you right for sodding about with them.'

Another time they took a boy's boots off and threw them on top of a furniture lorry, so that the boy had to get a ladder to climb on top to retrieve them. The fitters then took the ladder away and started rocking the lorry until the boy was screaming to be let down.

Fortunately I never suffered any such experiences.

At Jessups we had a man who did the general tidying up of the garage. He was a bit backward and he always wore a collar and tie. The amount of times his tie would dangle in the oil trays or in something that would cut bits off of it until he had just the knot left, would always make us laugh.

One day the boys joked that a girl passing on a bus had noticed him and left her phone number for him to ring her. But instead they gave him the London Zoo number and told him to ask for a 'Miss Lion'. The person answering said, 'The only Miss we have here is Miss Fortune.'

I was sixteen when I started my apprenticeship, and over the course of five years I went right through the trade: engine shop, stripping and rebuilding engines, rebores, chassis shop, brakes, steering, differentials, electrics and the stores. I also attended college once a week for the City and Guilds. I passed the first two years, but failed the third because my schooling was very interrupted by the war.

There were five boy apprentices, myself being the youngest. We were a mixed bunch. Some of us knew the theory, but could not do the practical, and some the opposite, of which I was one.

At eighteen I applied for my licence and went with a fitter in the service van to the test station in West Ham Lane. You had to park in the road opposite which had a small gradient and my fitter suggested I practised coming out of it onto the high road. I stalled it three times so he said, 'We will face the van downhill.'

The driving examiner called me out and after I had read some car number plates we started off. We came up the road parallel to the one we had been in and fortunately there was nothing coming along West Ham Lane, so I did not stall.

Back at the test station I was informed that I had passed. I wanted to take the 'L' plates off and drive back to Jessups so that they could all see I had passed, but my fitter (appropriately named Arthur Carr, or, 'Arfer Car') said, 'I will drive.' I was choked with disappointment.

I was working on a Bedford lorry once, adjusting the brakes, when the driver said, 'My brakes are pulling to one side. Could it be an air lock?'

I asked him what he meant and he said, 'You know, an air lock in the brake fluid.' I looked puzzled and explained that he had cable brakes. He then said, 'Oh! I have been putting brake fluid in!' I didn't bother to ask where.

I had a similar experience when a driver told me he kept blowing bulbs in the side light. I went to the stores to get a twelve-volt bulb and it lit with no problems. He was surprised, so I had to inform him that the vehicles had all been upgraded to twelve-volt systems and were not six any more.

One evening when we were sitting indoors having tea my father told us a story about one of his workmates. Apparently, as my father finished work, the chap needed a push to help start his car, so my father lent a hand and the car started. My father said, 'Why don't you use the starting handle? Then you wouldn't have to keep pushing it.'

'I would, but it's broken,' he said.

So my father offered, 'In the morning, I will see the blacksmith and get you a new one made up.'

The next day the blacksmith went and measured up and made a new starting handle. After a few days my father asked the chap if the starting handle had been a help. He replied, 'No, not really. Someone stole the car.' What luck!

One of the customers was Erith Builders Merchants. They had about twelve O- and S-model Bedfords that were replaced about every two years and two or three came in for servicing every week. The drivers would leave the vehicles for one of the older boys to deliver to their depot at Leytonstone after work.

I had my eye on this job, so when the boy left I told the foreman that I lived in Leytonstone and could deliver the vehicles, so I got the job (I actually lived quite a fair distance away from it).

One afternoon I ran into the boy who had lived upstairs of our old flat. He told me that his friend had bought a Morris Eight Saloon and was taking driving lessons and when he passed his test he was going to take three friends to Devon.

He then came over a few days later to tell me that his friend had failed his test. He asked me what I thought about coming with them to do the driving, as the holiday was already booked. I had to ask him how he thought we would get five blokes with their luggage into a Morris Eight, but he had that covered. 'We will send our luggage down by rail, and it will just be us five in the car,' he said. I agreed, so in July we took our luggage to the station and sent it to the Wheatsheaf pub in Tiverton.

The car found the hills rather a struggle, so sometimes the others had to get out so I could drive up the hill on my own. I would go a little further on and stop and lie in the sun until they reached me. They called me all sorts of things, but I said, 'Well, the driver has to get his rest!' It was all good fun.

I remember the pub having an arch which you had to go through to get into the courtyard and a hundred yards further along the road there being a roundabout. Every evening after we had been out I did two circuits of the roundabout and then shot straight through the arch; the boys loved it.

We were out one day, going along the country lanes, when I got stuck behind a local who was plodding along. I wanted to get by him, but I could tell the Morris was not really up to the job. Eventually I started to overtake until we were almost racing him, when suddenly I noticed a little humpbacked bridge coming up fast. I thought to myself, 'Well, I have got this far, so I will have to carry on,' and we both went over the bridge together.

Unluckily, waiting the other side was a speed cop on his motor bike, who came straight after me. When we stopped he looked at us and said, 'London boys.' I admitted that we were and he said sternly, 'What you have to realise is, the roads here are not like yours in London, they are very narrow and you took a chance overtaking that car on a bridge. Now enjoy your holiday and don't try foolish things like that again. Be on your way.'

I sit here now and cannot think what possessed me to do such a stupid thing. I can only think that I was young and senseless.

In the evenings we would sit chatting to the locals and playing darts with a few beers. I really enjoyed that holiday.

I had good friends away from work as well. I always remember going to the cinemas and paying for the dearest seats just so we could roam about looking for girls. One time my mate kept tapping the girl in front of me on the shoulder until she turned round to me and told me to stop it. I tried to explain that it wasn't me, but she would not have it. He kept on at it, until suddenly she swung her handbag back over her head and hit me so hard it nearly knocked me out. I do not know what was in it but it bloody hurt. I really shouted at him then.

We were out one night when that same friend told me he had some dope. He showed me what looked like bird seed in some grease-proof paper, saying he had bought it off one of his workmates. He proceeded to roll a cigarette out of it, even though he did not smoke. I couldn't stop laughing, 'You'll start chirping in a moment!' I said.

An ice-cream parlour opened in the Leytonstone high road, right by the bus stop. One evening my father got off the bus on his way home from work and by chance met an old friend from his Bouts Tillotson days and found out that he was actually the proprietor of the parlour. They got chatting and my father offered to help out with selling the ice-cream by riding a three-wheel tricycle with the fridge box on the front all around Canning Town.

This was a fair few miles and he would come home very tired after peddling the heavy bike. When they eventually bought an old Bedford ambulance they took the windows out of the body and the rear doors off and put a fridge box in the back. This was much better, but my father had to keep getting in and out of the van when he was stopped for ice-cream sales. So he suggested that I could go with him. I would drive the van and improve my driving skills, while he sat in the back and sold the ice-cream. In the evenings we would go all round Canning Town and Woolwich selling ice cream together.

There were always local children trying to sit on the van while it drove around. One particular evening my father kept telling the children to get off the step, but they wouldn't. So I thought that if I started off quickly, it would chuck them off. I saw that my father was sitting on the freezer box looking out the back so I revved up and slipped the clutch and started off as quickly as I could. I then looked round to see my father hanging on to the back-door supports. I had nearly shot him out the back of the van!

He shouted out, 'What the bloody hell was that all about?'

'I was trying to get the children off the step,' I said.

He laughed, 'I thought you were in a hurry to get home and were practising your clutch starts!' he said.

One evening in September we all piled into the van to go and see the Southend illuminations. After a nice evening we started on our way home, but when we got to Vange near Basildon we got a puncture. With no spare wheel we had to sleep in the van, and with no windows or back doors we nearly froze.

In the morning a lady from one of the nearby bungalows came out with tea and biscuits and asked if she could help. My father requested the use of her phone to ask a friend to bring us a spare wheel on the train.

So we waited for him to arrive with the spare and when it was fitted we left for home; it was mid-day by then. Back then it had seemed like we were in the outback and miles from home, but today we live fairly near Basildon and it's actually no distance from London at all. Vange is just down the road from where we live and it brings back memories every time I pass by.

Around the corner from where we lived was the manager of the Kings Cross coach station, and when he found out my father had a PSV licence (Public Service Vehicle) he offered him a part-time job driving the coaches at weekends.

The coaches would bring servicemen home to London

from Norfolk. They would be parked up until the Monday, so the station made use of them by contracting them out to Grey-Green Coaches. My mother was pleased, saying 'At least you will get paid for what you do' (he was not paid for his help selling the ice-cream). So my father began his part-time work, later finding work nearer to home with Galleon (or Essex County Coaches as it was then).

On most weekends my mother and father would go to the local for a drink, often coming home with their friends, one of whom was a pianist, which allowed them to have a good 'knees up'. I was a bit shy and not really a party person, but on one occasion I sat talking to a young girl named Pat all night. A few days later my cousin came round and said that Pat had bought a blouse, which she then decided she did not like, so had given it to her. When my cousin asked Pat how much she wanted for it she said, 'Nothing, if you can get me a date with Al.'

A friend and I went round to her house and were invited in by her father. He told us she was out dancing at Leyton baths, although she had told him to expect me and to tell her when she arrived home. He was a lorry driver who worked for Metropolitan Transport, which served the International Food and Kearley and Tonge stores, in Devon and Somerset. I got on well with Pat's dad mainly because we were both motor enthusiasts. I used to listen for hours about his journey work as a lorry driver, the nights away from home and the comradeship of the long distance drivers, although Pat's mum did not see it as quite so exciting.

The following day I went back to her house and Pat and I went out on a date. We carried on seeing a lot of each other for a whole year, until my call-up.

At Jessups I had become very friendly with a young car salesman who had just started. He couldn't drive and asked me if I would take him out in the evenings with the service van to give him driving lessons. So he, his girlfriend, Pat and I used to have pleasant evenings driving round Epping Forest, always stopping for a drink somewhere.

Every year we had the firm's outing to the coast (a beano) where everything was paid for by Jessups: beer, sandwiches and cigarettes for the smokers (naturally Chippy was the main smoker and made sure there were none left at the end of the day) and, when we arrived at the coast, a lunch in one of the restaurants.

However, I was more concerned with the coaches and drivers, who were mainly from Timpsons, of Catford. I watched the driver like a hawk, anticipating the engine noise and when he was going to change gear; in my mind I was driving it for him.

I was able to do plenty of driving around the garage, but it was not enough for me; I wanted to get out on the road. Some evenings I would ride miles on my bike trying to find my way to different places, reading road maps to get a general lay-out of where places were and in what direction.

All these things about my time at Jessups took place over six and a half years and I still remember all of them well now.

At eighteen I had the option of doing national service immediately, or of finishing my apprenticeship and then going when I completed it at twenty-one. I opted for the latter. When the national service boys came home on leave they would ask me which service I wanted to go in for. I would say I was not really bothered, as I only had to do two years. They would press upon me not to go in for the

Army with all that web bulling, but to join the Merchant
Navy so that I could see the world and buy the silk shirts,
ties and clothes they got from abroad. But I was not convinced. I was then told to go in the RAF, as there was not
as much spit and polish. So I chose the RAF. I wanted an
easy life for the two years.

Pat's mum proved her forcefulness at this time. When
the time came to do my national service she suggested that
Pat and I should get married, as then we could put my
married service pay away for my 'demob' and have enough
money for a deposit on a house. I suppose this was logical
thinking, but I had not even considered marriage yet and
didn't propose to Pat. Perhaps Pat's mum had wanted to
get rid of her daughter.

Chapter 3

National Service

I had to be assessed on my ability to enter the RAF and this took me to Woodford. I was given several tests, such as fitting variously shaped blocks into the corresponding holes and a general intelligence exam.

A few weeks later I was accepted; it was December 1953. To be kitted out I had to go to RAF Cardington, Bedfordshire, where the big Zeppelin hangers were. I was then posted to West Kirby on the Wirral for 'square-bashing'. It was the usual thing, plenty of bull: marching, drilling, running here and there and fatigues.

The PTI (physical training instructor) was always trying to get the best squad onto the parade ground and keep you on your toes, especially with kit inspections. Two of us were put on fatigues on one occasion and had to go to the camp telephone exchange to tidy up. But when we got there the regular Erks (slang for RAF personnel) said, 'Don't worry, make yourself some tea and toast.' From then I thought, 'I'll be a telephonist if they can make their own tea and toast.' We were always starving.

Food was a big motivator for us in those days. The station often wanted blood donors, but we would refuse, saying, 'We haven't got enough blood ourselves!' That was until they told us that you get tea and biscuits for it, then there was a mad panic to give blood.

We had the usual slagging off: our kit getting thrown about, people asking if you were pressing your uniform with a knife and fork. We had to buff our boots until you could see your face in them and shape our beret hats so we looked 'something like an airman' before we were let out in public. There were pieces of felt on the barrack floor so as not to scratch it.

In the winter months, with all the bad weather and snow, we certainly didn't have to be told to keep moving. We rose at six o'clock and did our ablutions, marching to the mess hall in thick snow. After breakfast we washed our cutlery in a big tank of boiling water.

We did our six weeks on the parade ground, marching and rifle drilling, and then had our passing-out parade. When we had a spot of leave, we would go home to recuperate.

Pat and I got married around this time, in St Johns Church, Stratford Broadway; I was in my uniform.

I was then posted to Weeton near Blackpool, for trade training as a motor mechanic and had to do their three-week course (even though in Civvy street I had been a full-time mechanic).

One weekend we were granted a thirty-six hour pass, so four of us decided to hitch-hike home to London. At dead on twelve o'clock, Saturday lunch-time, we stood outside the camp gates with our thumbs raised, homeward bound. It was a struggle with four of us, I think the only reason we were offered lifts was because I had stayed in uniform. We used every type of transport you could name: cars, lorries, dust carts, vans, and night trunkers. Late in the evening we decided the best option was to split up as we had to be back at camp for Monday morning. I carried on, reaching London in the early hours of the Sunday morning. I then had to wait for the Underground to start so that I could get home to Stratford, arriving home at about nine o'clock. Thankfully, my father paid my fare back to camp; I would never have made it in time if I had hitched again.

While at Weeton I approached the driving school's Chief Instructor and asked if I could do the driving course as soon as possible. However, he told me that I had to pass my Mechanics course and then spend six months with my new unit before they would send me back to do the three-week driving course. I had different ideas. Every day after my lessons I would go round to see the Squadron Leader in charge of the driving school and pester him to let me do the driving course there and then, insisting I could do the whole three-week course in one day.

'Right then!' he said. 'If you are so sure you can do it, we will take you out for a test. Have you driven a QL Bedford troop carrier?' Well, I had to admit, I hadn't driven a troop carrier before, though I had served an apprenticeship with Bedfords. He told me to come back tomorrow for the test; I couldn't wait.

The next day I went to the driving school and there stood the wagon with an instructor. He took me all round Blackpool for two hours and as soon as I returned he told me I had passed. Despite this good news, I still had two more lessons to complete, one being Mechanics (which I was already doing and did pass) and the third being Theory, which entailed map reading and the Highway Code, but I passed this also; I was away! When I passed out as Driver Mechanic the driving staff told me that it had never been done before. I was proud to have made a piece of history.

While I was training at Weeton there were a few

amusing incidents. For example, Flight Sergeants and Chief Technicians were basically the same rank, and so the regulars would often use abbreviations, such as 'Flight' or 'Chief'.

On one occasion on the parade ground, the Chief Technician was talking to the man beside me who kept calling him 'Chiefy'. He was not amused, saying to the guy, 'Do not keep calling me Chiefy. What do you think I am? A Red Indian? My rank is Chief Technician, not Chiefy.'

I had to hide my smile.

When we finished the course we were allowed to give a preference as to where we wanted to be posted. I hoped for North Weald in Essex, and a pal of mine wanted to go near his home at Eastbourne. It was just our luck that I got Eastbourne and he went to North Weald.

We couldn't have changed even if we had tried, because at Eastbourne they only wanted qualified drivers like me, whereas my friend as still just a Mechanic.

We were a satellite station. Wartling, near Hastings, was our parent station and we were all billeted in new council houses in Eastbourne just outside the town, near to the new hospital of today, two to a room.

We had Standard Vanguard Pickups and staff cars, Austin two- and three-tonners, QL Bedford troop carriers and Bedford coaches. These were used for transporting radar operators to Beachy Head, a radar station known as the top site. The staff was made up of about twelve drivers and one mechanic (who did nothing because all the repairs had to go to Wartling).

It was like a holiday camp; we had sugar bowls on the mess tables, cut bread, butter dishes, and as much food as you liked. It was heaven, totally different from the 'square-bashing' weeks. Working on transport made us everyone's friend; we could walk into the mess and have something to eat any time; we walked round the camp like kings. If anyone upset us they knew we could refuse to wait at the station on weekends to give them lifts back to camp. We would give lifts to town and help in any way, but our main job was transporting the radar operators to the Beachy Head radar site.

We usually had more drivers than vehicles and on occasions, when we had a visit from the Air Marshals, our corporal would say, 'Have a day in town, if he sees we are over-staffed someone will get posted.'

I passed the special coach driving licence, which meant that I could drive all the vehicles on camp. I was then promoted to LAC (Leading Aircraftman), the lowest rank for specialist vehicle drivers. A few days into this I was on duty and had to take a signal to the top site. On arriving I went into the guardroom and spoke to the SP (the military service police) and enquired how they fitted ninety people down here in this small room. He said, 'Oh, is this your first time inside here? I will take you down to the watch rooms.' When I went down it was like Star Wars; there were underground tunnels and rooms with all the screens for the radar operators. I could not believe that all this was inside the Beachy Head cliffs.

The corporal in charge of the MT (Motor Transport) section ordered me and a fellow airman to take the Austin 5-tonner to Wartling to pick up the rations. On the way back we stopped at a local café and had sat chatting for some time when I noticed across the hedgerow that a girl was watching us.

I said to my fellow airman, 'Don't look now, but there is

a girl clocking us across the hedgerow.' When he saw her he started waving.

'Don't do that,' I said, but the girl was already coming round the corner to speak with us. I noticed straight away she was pregnant. On this particular occasion I was riding shotgun, so I wound down the window and she said, 'Hello, do you come from the camp in Eastbourne?'

I didn't want to be caught out with that, so I said, 'No, love, we don't come from anywhere round here.'

To which she replied, 'I didn't know if you knew my husband because he is at Eastbourne.' I thought, 'Blimey, we have been eyeing up the C.O.'s wife!'

A few days later our corporal called us into the office and said, 'Why did you tell my wife you did not come from here?'

I thought, 'Thank God it was not the C.O.'s wife.'

'We were only kidding her up,' I said (I did not like to tell him the real reason). In fact I got very friendly with him and his wife, spending a lot of time at his married quarters when I was off duty. Some weekends when I was on duty they would invite Pat down for the weekend and when their baby was born we would baby-sit for them.

On another occasion while on the ration run, I was again riding shotgun and we stopped at the same café. There were road-works this time and my driver pulled right up to their warning board. 'We can't leave it here, it's obscuring the road-works board,' I said.

'Oh, it will be all right,' he said. We came out and sat chatting for a while, forgetting all about the board. So when we started off, he ran right over it, smashing it to a pulp. The men working down the hole were shouting and waving their arms madly at us as we cleared off. I don't think they thought much of us!

I remember when the railway decided to go on strike. Service personnel were told to get to their nearest camp where transport would be laid on to get them back to their respective camps. The corporal called to me and said, 'Hornchurch is close to where you live, isn't it?'

'Yes, it is,' I said.

So he said, 'Friday evening you have to take a Squadron Leader to RAF Hornchurch and then you can go home for the weekend,' which I did.

On my way back to Eastbourne I picked up an army soldier thumbing for a lift (there were no roundels on the car so you would not know it was an air force car). He could not thank me enough as it was so late in the evening that he had been worried about getting back to camp on time.

He kept calling me sir, which I told him to stop, as I was a serviceman myself and in fact this was an RAF staff car. He seemed quite shocked that I had pulled up for him, as we were supposed to be rivals. We chatted all the way about the difference between the two services until we arrived at the camp gates.

I only came into contact with the Army once more during my time in the national service. I wasn't a sports person, but I knew that in the forces, if you were a sports person or indeed a musician, you were made. Wednesday afternoons was sports day and so I always volunteered to be the duty driver.

This particular Wednesday our football team was playing the Army and on arrival at the camp we were greeted by one of the football players, who told us that after the game we would have a lovely spread laid on. I thought, 'This will be great,' because in the RAF we were always treated like lords with things like this.

However, we agreed that we'd better not go into the mess until it was cleared of soldiers, so there would be no ill feeling.

'Bring it on,' I thought.

We lost the match. When it was over we waited for the mess to empty and then went in. I was very surprised; to start with, the cooks looked like they had been cleaning the chimney. Their whites had soot all over them (probably from the field kitchen). We were given a plate and told to stand in a queue. I received two sparrow's eggs, a few chips, beans and a chipolata sausage, two slices of bread with one piece of butter and a slab of cake. I tried to spread the piece of butter on to the bread but it would only cover one slice, so I asked, 'Please sir, can I have some more butter?' In no uncertain terms I was told, 'Clear off, you're in the army here.'

We rushed back to camp at the double, and went straight to the mess for something to eat. I was so glad I had applied for the air force.

On one of my weekends at home I sat talking to my father-in-law about transport. I always saw him as a gentleman driver, everything had to be perfect. I remember him telling me that he went out in his little car once (an Austin A 30) and as he went round a corner some boys spat on it, so he drove round the block and came back. The boys hadn't noticed, so he pulled up and grabbed one of them, making him wipe it off. You could not do that today, of course.

If it rained he would put his car in the garage and leather it off. In fact, if it rained, he would walk rather than get his car wet. He never allowed it to stand wet over-night, he never raced the engine and if you followed him, you wondered if you would ever get to where you were going he was such a careful driver. He always treated the vehicle with pride and that went for his lorry too.

He was now driving for British Road Services and was on a GEC (General Electrical Company) contract, carrying radio and electrical parts to Birmingham. On Mondays he would load at the Kingsway Central in London and stop over night at Daventry; Tuesday he would go on to Birmingham and tip his load, then he would reload and head back to Daventry and on Wednesday he would go home. He would then be back out Thursday to Saturday.

He told me that Metropolitan Transport had had a state-of-the-art workshop, with washing and greasing facilities, but when British Road Services took over they had shut the depot and put them all on the Hackney Marshes, so that when you parked up you had six inches of mud to contend with. He was not happy with BRS and often said they had pushed us back twenty years. It was not long after this that he applied for the buses.

While I was still serving I was once on a night shift where I had to take the watch change up to top site. We loaded up and were going round a bend in a country lane (the headlights were nothing to write home about) when I saw something in front and swerved to avoid it. We stopped and three of us got out to find a drunk asleep in the road; we picked him up and put him on the grass verge. We carried on to the top site and informed the police. On the return journey we saw the police looking for him; we stopped to help, but he was nowhere to be found.

I recall one moment of madness when, coming down a steep hill, I knocked the gearbox into neutral so that I could coast along merrily on my own. When I started to approach some traffic lights I pressed on the brakes, but suddenly the engine cut out as the servo (brake assistance) came into force. I had to restart the engine, so with my right foot on the brake I tucked my left foot under my right foot and on to the accelerator. I restarted the engine and dropped it back into gear and, with not a moment to spare, stopped at the lights. I never coasted again.

I was in the mess one day when a guy behind me tapped me on the shoulder, and asked, 'How old are you?'

'Twenty-two,' I stated.

'You're losing your hair,' he said.

I admitted that I was. He then said that he was studying at the London hospital with a scalp specialist and if I wanted, he would try and save me from more hair loss. 'In for a penny in for a pound,' I thought and agreed to see him the next day.

When I got to his billet I could not believe it, it looked like a pharmacy. First, he rubbed different oils in my hair and then massaged my scalp. He did this every day when we finished our duties and at the end he said, 'I have made you up some potion with added perfume. Use it every day and you should see some improvement.' So I paid and left.

I walked in the next morning and all the Motor Transport guys were sniffing, saying, 'Who smells like a pox doctor's clerk?' When they found out it was me they said, 'Brylcream is all right, but get that crap off.' So I do not know if it would ever have worked. We did have a few Brylcream Boys in the squad, who would be 'tarting' themselves up all day, looking in the car mirrors.

I was on a train going home one weekend when a lady opposite me asked, 'Going back, son?'

I said, 'No, going home.'

She said, 'Where is the RAF in Eastbourne then?' When

I told her Beachy Head, she said, 'Oh, when you see an airman you associate him with an aerodrome.'

I laughed and said, 'I have not seen an aerodrome. In fact, when I see an airplane I have to ask if it is one of ours.'

I was once detailed to go to Dumfries in Scotland and meet with a party of airmen, to pick up one of the new Standard Vanguard staff cars. I was to drive to Boscombe Down in Wiltshire, where there was a big meeting with all the Air Staff and Members of Parliament. Once there we were to fulfil all their needs.

Some landed in aircraft but one cocky pilot tried to turn too short and crashed. He was not hurt, only his ego was damaged.

I was detailed to pick up a Member of Parliament (I was not that interested in who he was) from the railway station and on the way to the camp he tried to small-talk me. He asked if I was regular, or national service and when I stated the latter he asked, 'How do you like it?' I replied that I felt I could be doing better things with my life than being here. He never said another word to me.

One dinner time in the mess I had mince pie and custard for my sweet, my favourite. I placed a large portion in my mouth, and felt something tough in there. I thought it must have been a stick from the fruit, so I sucked all the fruit from it. When I looked at it I realised it was an inch-long rusty nail. The Sergeant was doing his rounds, shouting, 'Any complaints?' So I called him over and said, 'Look at this, Sarge.'

He looked at me and said, 'Don't shout it out, because they will all want one, but go and get another piece.'

'No thanks,' I replied.

I was promoted to SAC (Senior Aircraftman) and one

evening I was detailed to be at the guardroom with a staff car. When I got there two officers were waiting with a hold-all. I was ordered to take them to the top site, but about a quarter of a mile before we reached the site I was told to stop. They got out and told me to turn the car round and wait for their return. When they came back after about an hour they told me to take them back to the camp.

The next morning all hell broke loose, apparently they had breached security and entered the compound, decorating the scanners with bunting. Of course, I could not have warned anybody, because I didn't know what they were up to. Security was put on full alert for a while after that.

On one of my weekends at home I visited Jessups to chat to my friends and met one of the apprentices who was also on leave from the RAF. He told me an amusing tale. He was attached to the airfield fire service and he had to go to another camp to pick up a stop cock. He said, 'I was carrying it in a sack on my back, crossing one of the main line railway stations in London, when I was stopped by two women SPs. They asked what I had in the sack, so I said a cock! They arrested me, escorted me back to camp and put me in front of the CO.'

The CO simply said, 'You could have been a bit more specific about it – seven days jankers.'

One night we were in the NAAFI having a drink and the topic of conversation was Merrydown rough cider and how lethal it was. We decided to try it, all having half a pint. Now, that may not sound a lot, but I remember coming out of the NAAFI doing handstands. I do not know what the rest were doing, but I was gone. I was in bed for two days after that. When we told the duty corporal, he called us a lot of 'nancy boys'.

So we replied, 'We will stand you a half pint, then you tell us what you think.' The challenge was on.

At ten o'clock we mustered at the guardroom for inspection, watching the corporal staggering all over the place and slurring his words awfully. The inspecting officer told us to take him away and out of his sight, otherwise he would charge him. We took him back to his billet and let him sleep it off; the next morning he said he couldn't remember a thing.

Much later when I was on the tankers, I use to pass the Merrydown cider factory on my way down to the south coast and would always think 'evil bloody stuff!'

On the late afternoon shift we were sometimes given coded messages, or 'signals' as they were called, to deliver to the top site; when we did this we often organised time trials to make it more interesting. When we got the signal, the SP at the camp security office put our time of leaving on a piece of paper and we raced up the hill in our Standard Vanguard staff cars flat out, getting the SP at the top to record our time of arrival. I suppose it was about ten miles each way, through country lanes, with a couple of hairpin bends. I believe some cheated, but it was exciting trying to beat everybody.

Before I left I made good friends with one of the crew who, when he came out, joined the Metropolitan Police Force. I was surprised because although he was a likeable fellow, he was one of those who were always in trouble. He even went on to become a high-ranking officer. He was noted for the brightly coloured ties he wore in the evenings and on days off; because of this he was nick-named Flash Gordon, or Flash.

I used to visit him and his wife at their home. Once he gave me a pint of lager and as I took a swig, it all ran down my chin and onto my shirt and tie, and he said, 'What is the matter with you? Can't you find your mouth?' I felt very embarrassed, but when I took another swig it happened again. This made him and his wife laugh a lot. Then I looked at the glass and all round the edge were tiny holes. My shirt and tie were soaked in lager. I had to drive home smelling of it – a good job I was not stopped.

I was twenty-three when my discharge came through. Looking back, my two years of national service were some of the best years of my life and also, my first time away from home alone.

Chapter 4

Marshall Taplow's

AFTER Christmas I returned to Jessups; it was as though I had never left.

However, problems began when I learnt more about one of the other employees. He was from the local cycle speedway team and had come to Jessups before I left for national service because he was out of work. His job was to strip the engines, putting all the nuts and bolts into big tin cans with holes in them and then lower them all into a big tank of degreaser fluid and boiling water. After a certain time he would take the parts out with the hoist and swing them over to a washing-off bay and wash the parts clean using a hose pipe. He would then give the fitters the parts to be reconditioned.

He had been exempt from the forces because of his flat feet. He was a great friend to me; we were always larking about and playing the fool, his party piece was taking off the singer Johnny Ray. One day, after I had returned from the service, we were talking about wages and I found out that he was earning more than me, even though I had served a five-year apprenticeship and he was only stripping engines.

I made an appointment to see the manager to discuss my grievance. He told me that I had been away for two years and in that time my friend had received numerous pay rises. So that was that. I had served five years as an apprentice for nothing.

A few weeks later I was talking to a neighbour who told me he worked for Marshall Taplow's, a subsidiary of Charrington Brewery, as a driver delivering wines and spirits to Charrington's public houses. His wages, including overtime (being on the road you never had a precise finishing time) were double what I was getting as a mechanic and the job was a sight cleaner. This was a bonus as my father was always moaning about the state of my hands and the grease and dirt that was ground into them, no matter how much I washed. My neighbour brought home an application form for me and I waited for the interview.

After I had been back at Jessups for about three months I received a call to attend an interview at Taplow's, who told me I could start whenever I was ready. So I said my goodbyes to Jessups and started my driving career at Taplow's.

A lot of things changed around this time. Pat and I had been renting a flat from my mother-in-law's brother in Ilford, but her father bought a large house in Forest Gate and offered us two of the upstairs rooms; so we moved in with them.

Taplow's used Bedford five-ton open-back lorries and Ford three-ton box vans; I was given a petrol Bedford. Charrington had bought out Page and Overton's Brewery in Croydon and some of the staff, instead of taking redundancy, opted to travel to Stratford, so I became friends with one of the men from Croydon, Nobby Clarke. He was a nice man, with no faults that I could find, and he became my checker, a role which involved putting the loads together before we headed off to deliver.

Our first job was to go to the warehouses in Wapping to pick up four pipes; I thought they must have been doing some building work. So we parked under a jib outside the warehouse and out came the biggest barrel I had ever seen, full of wine. We loaded four of these until there was no more room on the lorry for anything else.

Nobby would get our orders for the day, which could be up to eighteen deliveries, and sort them out in order. He had been doing this for years and knew every pub south of the river Thames. Having sorted them he would start getting the pub order up, stacking the crates in boxes of three; I would then truck them and stack them on the lorry. My father had taught me how to rope and sheet, which proved very useful, although Nobby had been doing it for years.

The pub orders would all be stacked on the loading bays by the inside staff and numbered so the checker knew that his orders were in that stack. Once loaded, we would set off on our way to pubs, off-licences and shops around south London, Kent, Surrey and Sussex. I was always happiest when we delivered a full load to the depots. I was amazed at the amount of wines and spirits some places took in; at Christmas some off-licences would take as much as fifteen tons, and that was without the beer. There would be three lorries waiting to unload and most of it would go upstairs in whatever space there was. We would all muck in but at the end of the day we would be exhausted.

Nobby was an old drayman so when he was in the cellars throwing out the crates and barrels I had to stand right back to try and catch them as they sailed right over my head. He was also a big drinker. If we had eighteen drops he would have at least ten pints, if not more, and when we finished at night he would go to the tap room and say, 'One for the road!' It was a good thing he travelled by rail. When I started with him, whenever the publicans asked if we wanted a drink or beer money he would always choose the drink, but after a time, when he knew I didn't drink while driving, he would opt for the money. Sometimes I would tell him to have a drink, which he always appreciated. I think he took quite a shine to me and was always saying how safe he felt with my driving. He was also as thin as a rake; I think all the exercise kept him slim.

The trouble with this job was that the transport manager kept me over the south side of London. On our way home he would always tell me to drop him off in Croydon, so I would have to come back on my own and unload the empties before I could leave. The only good thing about this was that I began to know the south of London and the south coast, especially their pubs, like the back of my hand.

When we had a delivery we would have to shout out the item names for someone to tick off, for example: 'A dozen bottles of Johnnie Walker! A dozen bottles of Booths Gin!'

One time I remember walking in and shouting, 'A dozen Noilly Prats!'

The woman from the off-licence whipped round and shouted, 'Come back here!' I walked back and she said, 'It's Noilly PRAAA . . . not Prat.'

So I said, 'Well, I'm just reading what it says on the bottle.'

Taplow's had their own brand of wines and spirits and always tried to sell them above the proprietary brands such as Johnnie Walker, Teachers, Booths, Gilbey's and the like. We were delivering to a village pub once and some old chaps were sitting at a table playing dominoes when, as we walked in, one of them shouted, 'Are you Taplow's with that Old Mountain Music?' (Taplow's whisky). I said that we were and in no uncertain terms he told me what I should do with it.

The governor laughed and said, 'The times I have given it to him in a Johnnie Walker bottle and he didn't know the difference.'

On another occasion we did a delivery to a pub which included a bottle of Dimple Haig. Dimple Haigs were like gold dust; in most pubs you would see the triangular-shaped bottle on the counter holding the coins for charity. I couldn't wait to give the landlord the good news. He said to me, 'I will only believe it when I see it.' So I rushed out to the lorry, but on my way back I tripped and fell and the bottle smashed on the floor in front of him; he was certainly not happy. I think he said some interesting words about my fall.

My checker was as true as they come. If we broke a bottle, he would sit all day nursing it and saving the contents until we returned to the depot. He would then give it to the supervisors and bank staff and they would say, 'Good old Nobby.' As soon as our backs were turned they would filter and drink it. I used to get quite annoyed about this at Christmas when we could have taken some home.

When he was away I would have younger checkers come with me and, if we were dry in the summer, they would open a bottle of cider. Or in the winter they would knock the top off a bottle of spirits and we would drink it. As long as we had the neck of the bottle intact it was all right. Often, when the loads were on the bank beside one another, the checkers would steal a case of the next load.

Of course the driver would never know, he would just be trucking it on the lorry and stacking it.

On one occasion my checker informed me that we had an extra case of Scotch on board and told me to pull up on the corner of a road for five minutes so that he could run down to the off-licence to see if they wanted to buy it. I soon discovered that I would never have made a get-away driver. I sat there looking at my watch, making sure I didn't go too early, when I looked up to see him shouting and waving his arms about at me to hurry up and bring it to him. When I got there he yelled, 'What were you waiting for?'

'Well, you said to wait five minutes!' I cried.

It was all cloak and dagger stuff. Another time I was in the yard washing down when one of the drivers approached me and said that a driver had been in an accident, so he had to take another truck to unload the goods, and asked if I would follow him in the service van. So I followed him until he stopped and told me to go into a café nearby where he would come back for me. He took the van and thirty minutes later he came back and said I could go back to the depot. I could only assume that he used the van to get rid of the extras.

I felt a bit bewildered when a few days later he gave me an envelope and said, 'That's for the other day.' When I opened it there was £50 inside. I tried to reason with him saying that I had not done anything, but he insisted on my keeping it and thanked me for my help; I suppose it was hush money.

When I got home I told Pat. She said, 'Either you give it back, or I will inform on you.' I was worried she would, so I gave her some money to buy herself something and no more was said.

We had to go to Wapping in East London to pick up some barrels of wine once. I pulled up at the jib, which came out of the top of the warehouse, and lowered the barrels onto the lorry. It seemed to be travelling at one hell of a speed and stopped about two inches from the lorry flooring.

'They must have done this before,' I thought, but at the same time I knew it would be bloody dangerous if you got in the way.

I looked over at my mate then and saw that his face was as black as the ace of spades, I fell about laughing and he started laughing too, as my face was apparently the same. It seemed that the barrels had been in the warehouse for months awaiting collection, so now they were outside in the rain all the dust that had gathered on the barrels was washed off right on top of us. There were more to come so we just had to stick it out; I bet the dock staff took great delight in our predicament. We got back after loading and had to have a good wash.

I had a nasty incident on a pub delivery once. We went into the yard to collect the empties and I picked up three empty cases of Babycham to place on the back of the lorry. As I went to walk away I felt a sharp sting and on looking at my finger I saw that one of the staples which held the strengthening wire round the crates was now embedded in my finger. It was about an inch long and had penetrated into the bottom of the top part of the finger, coming out at the top.

Nobby grimaced and said, 'We'll go to the hospital.' The guv'nor also came over and offered to run us there, coming back for us when we were done.

I was seen by Accident and Emergency, but they didn't have anything strong enough to get it out, so they sent to the maintenance department for some pliers. It took one hell of a time to remove. I was out of my senses.

Another traumatic experience occurred when I was on my way home one night after having dropped off Nobby in Croydon. I cut round the back of Tower Bridge through a narrow road and approached green traffic lights in Commercial Road. I then heard fire engines coming from my left, so I stopped. The first engine driver indicated that he was turning right to come round past me, which he did, but the second engine misjudged it so that suddenly I was in the way. With an almighty bang his off-side rear collided with my off-side front, tearing a big gash in the side of his engine. 'The bugger's not stopped,' I thought, but one of the firemen dropped off and explained that if it was capable the engine had to continue to the shout and he would do the necessary paper work. I only had front-damage to the lorry so I managed to get back to the yard.

Nobby was a DIY fanatic and for weeks he had us searching the empties for a particular bottle he wanted for the coving in his house (I don't think it would be like the coving you get today, but then I am no decorator). It was exactly the right shape and diameter, he told me, for the plastering. Eventually we found one. Some time later when I dropped him off he invited me in to see the finished room. It was like a palace! I could not believe all that he had done.

He told me that he had plastered the top of the wall where it met the ceiling, rolling it to get the coving; now that is what I call DIY. He had also flushed the doors, which was all the rage then.

I had been at Taplow's for about fifteen months and was getting fed up with always being south of the Thames. I had nothing personal against Nobby, I was just fed up with the same routine. I fancied working the Essex side for a change. I spoke with the manager and asked if I could have a change. 'No, you can't,' he said.

So I spoke to my father and father-in-law and they both suggested trying the buses, so I thought, 'Why not?'

Chapter 5

London Transport

I went up to Marylebone London Transport head-quarters and was directed to a large room with desks and an usher standing in the doorway. The usher gave me the appropriate forms to fill in for bus driving and directed me to one of the desks.

Another fellow came in wanting to be a bus conductor. He was given the forms and told to sit. He had a friend with him and when the usher asked him what he wanted he said, 'Nothing.'

The usher said, 'Well, wait outside then.'

But the man said he couldn't, 'I have to help him with the forms because he can't read or write,' he said.

The usher wasn't amused and said, 'I suppose you are going to stand on the back punching his tickets for him; he's got an interview, but no job.'

I went in and had the interview, but they only wanted trolleybus drivers and I wanted to drive diesels, so I said I was not interested. However, when I came home my father-in-law said, 'It's only for a short time and then we're changing over to Routemasters.' So he talked me into accepting it.

I went back and told them I had changed my mind and so they gave me an appointment to go to Chiswick. When I got there I was told to sit outside on some benches and someone would come and see me. I sat watching some buses tearing round a circuit and could see that they were going to approach me. As they came forward they went into an almighty skid; I did not know whether to brave it out or to run. I later found out that I was sitting in front of the skid pan. A chap came out and took me for a test drive in a van to see what my chances were. After a short while he said I would do and gave me a date to pick up the uniforms.

I then met about twelve other recruits all going to different garages and we sorted out who was going where. It turned out that there were two drivers going to West Ham with me, one of whom lived in the next road to me, so I brought him home in my car; his name was John, and he had been driving for Heaslip Transport. I found him to be a bit of a braggart but it did not worry me.

I gave Taplow's a week's notice. The manager said he was sorry to see me go, and if it did not turn out as expected then there was always a job for me there, which was nice to know. The fitter was also sorry to see me go, saying that the Bedford had been returning a good petrol consumption while I had been there.

We reported to the West Ham bus garage on the Monday morning and were introduced to our instructor. He was a middle-aged man and rather portly. He took us through the shed to a waiting bus with 'L' plates and 'Driver Under Instruction' at each end. He took us inside the bus and told us to sit down, explaining that he didn't want to know what we had been driving before as this was something totally different. He carefully explained how to drive the bus, but at the end John said, 'Give me five minutes in the cab and I'll show you a thing or two.'

I could not believe what he had just said; I wondered

whether he was joking, but it seemed that he was dead serious. I myself never said what I could or could not do, even in the RAF. That way other people could be impressed if they wanted to be, but it didn't matter if they weren't.

The instructor wasn't amused, 'Why is there always one?' he asked. 'Right, we will have you first, get in the cab.' If there had been a hole big enough I think John would have wanted it to swallow him up. The instructor made him look a complete fool.

The instructor told him to look above his head to find two main switches with levers; these brought power to the bus from the overhead wiring so that we could move. He explained that we had two pedals, one was the power and the other was the footbrake. You had to knock the main switches in and push the power pedal down slowly while letting the handbrake off until the bus moved, and then come off the pedal so that the bus would coast. If you wanted to move further you gave the pedal another press and you were away.

The instructor told us that at some time during our training we would encounter a loss of power, either from the poles coming off, or because we built up the power too fast so that it blew out the two main switches. When that happened we just had to knock the switches back in. We must have been good drivers because we didn't blow the main switches, but maybe that was because we were so frightened of the thing.

There were three of us training together. John and I had driven lorries before, whereas the other chap only had experience of cars. It soon became apparent that he needed more instruction than we did – so he did most of the driving.

When we were not driving we stood on the back of the bus because when you pulled up at a bus stop, even though we had 'L' plates and 'Driver Under Instruction' on the bus, people saw a red bus and wanted to get on. We had a strap going across the platform but people would still climb over it. I used to think that even if it was a red post office van people would try to get in.

Our uniform included a cap with a white top. One day while driving, John shouted to the instructor, 'I've got no power!'

The instructor shouted, 'What did I tell you on the first day about power loss?' He was referring to the light which had gone out above the driver, indicating the power to the bus. 'Did you hear that bang?' he asked.

'Was that the main switches?' John asked.

The instructor nodded that it was and John said, 'Oh, I thought it would have been worse than that!'

'I don't know about that, John', said the instructor. 'Wait until you look at the top of your hat!'

We had three weeks training and route learning, but I already knew all of the routes because I used to travel with my father so much when he was on the buses. However, entering the depot was a nightmare as there were dead sections all along it, so the instructor would shout, 'Power, off, power, off, power, off', so that you could coast through them. Dead sections occurred at wiring junctions and sections, and so as well as driving you had to watch the wiring. When approaching dead sections you had to come off the power, if you did not, because you were using pulling power, there would be a big flash as you hit them.

Entering the depot was a nightmare because of all the dead sections; I would come in at a gallop and just hope I had enough speed to see me to my parking allocation.

Sometimes I didn't time it right and had to try and get some more power; if you happened to hit a dead section the depot would light up like a Christmas tree.

We had our final test at Aldgate bus terminus. It was decided that I would bring the bus out of the terminus and along Commercial Road, then somewhere along Barking Road the driver with less experience would drive the straight bit, and then John would take it to Barking. When we arrived we were informed we had all passed.

After our passing-out I did not see much of the less experienced driver, although I did hear he was forever having accidents and that he eventually met a conductress and they transferred to Barking garage.

The only thing that worried me was keeping to a time-table. On our first day on duty John had an early shift and I had an afternoon shift, so in the morning I waited at the bus stop for him to arrive. I walked to the front (the cabs had a drop-down window so that you could lean in and talk to the driver) and asked how he was getting on. He said, 'I keep catching up with the bus in front, but at the moment it's all good.' I left him and waited my turn. I had to 'take my bus off' (slang for starting your duty) at Plaistow Broadway and I was worried. The passengers would take it for granted that the driver knew what he was doing and would not understand that it was your first day.

I would ideally have liked to take a bus out from the depot, but I was detailed to take over on the road. I saw a conductor standing with his duty box and asked him if he was doing the next duty, which he was. I apologised to him, explaining that it was my first day, so not to expect miracles. 'You've drawn the short straw,' I said.

He laughed: 'We all have a first day. Here are a few tips: firstly, forget the time board, don't even bother with it, the inspectors on the road know you are about so they are looking for you. If we are running late they will turn us short. Secondly, take it easy and stay out of trouble.' My mind was put at rest.

The bus drew up and I could see the passengers sitting there looking to the front. I wished they would look the other way, though they did not seem concerned with the change of driver at all. The driver getting off informed me that everything was OK, so I jumped in and adjusted my seat. After the bell rang I was away.

To say I had a perfect day would certainly be an over-statement. When you gave the bus the first notch on the power pedal, being an electric motor, the twin back axles would jump, sending a shock (not electric) through the bus that gave it a jolt. My father had said that to overcome this you should keep hold of the handbrake, releasing it once you had the first notch release, ensuring a smooth take-off.

I wanted to impress the conductor by giving him a good ride (if you want to know if anyone is a good driver you ask a conductor) and so I held the handbrake on all my starts and kept my braking smooth. However, this meant that I was losing a lot of time. In the end I thought 'sod the handbrake' and did not even wait for the bell. I would pull up at the stop and watch the mirrors inside and out. It was a case of whether the conductor could get to the bell before I was away.

I was starting to make up time, but when I came round Maryland point I saw that two cars had collided. I had to shout to them to get out the way as I was running late. I got past that obstacle only to find another.

The wiring was always set for straight, so if you wanted to turn left you had to pull what was known as the 'frog'. The frog was a lever attached to a pole which hung down from the wires which, when the conductor got out of the bus to pull it, changed the direction of the wiring. They would also have to watch to make sure the trolleys cleared the wire junction.

As I came to West Ham church I noticed some children were standing by the frog, but thought nothing of it. I carried straight on and suddenly the light went out in the cab. I pulled up and got out to find the children had pulled the frog as I passed them, so that while I was going straight, my trolleys had gone around the corner to the left.

This ended my first day. In the evening I went round to John's house and we compared notes.

I had been on the buses for a week when I found myself waiting for my bus at the Boleyn pub. On my bus's arrival the inspector asked me where my conductor was; I replied that I didn't know. Then the next bus came up and the inspector said, 'Take the sticks down and transfer the people onto the bus behind.'

I stood there for some time while the inspector tried to find out what had happened to the lost conductor. The inspector was getting exasperated, 'He has collected his box from the depot, so I haven't got a clue where he is.' A short time later the inspector explained, 'It's the conductor's first day and he was waiting at Silvertown; the inspector at Silvertown has told him to get down to the Boleyn pronto.' He arrived moments later, full of apologies. The inspector simply said, 'Right, put your trolleys up and when you get to Stratford the inspector there will put you right.'

So off we went, only to catch up with the bus in front. I couldn't pass because of the trolleys on their bus, so the conductor in front kept shouting at me, 'Lift your bloody foot up!' to make me slow down. He did not realise that we had got out of sequence and could not do much about the situation. We then arrived at Stratford to find that the inspector would not let me on the bus stand, telling me to go round again; we were on what the drivers called 'the wall of death'.

Stratford was the starting point; we went along West Ham Lane to the church, left through Plashet Road (where the children pulled the frog on my first day), turned right down Green Street to the Boleyn, left along the Barking Road to East Ham Town Hall, left through the high street, and left through Plashet Grove, back to the bank, then through Plashet Road and to Stratford. Then we had to do it all again the other way round.

We kept going around until we were giddy. Every time we got to Stratford the inspector would not let us on the stand. Eventually I think even he had had enough, especially as we kept catching up with the bus in front who were not happy either. So he called a truce and let us on the bus stand. The inspector told us to take the trolleys down and go round to the café for a cup of tea and he would put us right when we came back.

He told me to turn at Findon Road; 'Where on earth is Findon Road?' I thought. There was a queue of people waiting to get on, so I started looking through the sight glass for the destination board. I had to stand up to do this, while continually winding the little handle to find *Findon Road*, but it was not on there, or at least I couldn't find it. When I looked at the people waiting to get on they were beckoning me to go up or down with the board; 'I don't know where the bloody hell I am going, so how do they know?' I thought. In the end I showed Bloomsbury on the board.

Away we went. The conductor was punching tickets to

his heart's desire and I was soaking in sweat. We were picking up and dropping off people all the way along; we were a bus crew after all. All the time I kept thinking, where is Findon Road? Then it suddenly came to me. I had to turn left and go down to the Romford Road and Findon Road would be on the corner.

When we got to the bank I sat studying the wiring and could see that there was none that would allow me to turn left, so I would have to pull the sticks down and go round on the battery, putting the trolley back up and then proceeding to Findon Road, so I shouted through the bus: 'All change!'

All the passengers had to get off and stand at the stop, so I sat there for a while and thought, if I go round to East Ham and then come along the Barking Road and turn right into Green Street I can go straight across because the wiring went straight down to Findon Road, brilliant! I shouted through the bus to my conductor to tell them to get back on, so my conductor shouted 'Right, all back on! My driver's decided to go for it.'

'What a bloody bus service this is,' the passengers were saying.

I called my conductor to come through the bus and told him that I couldn't find Findon Road on the destination board, so he would have to shout out 'Findon Road only'.

We eventually got to Findon Road and sat there laughing hysterically to ourselves. 'I'll certainly remember my first day,' he said 'and your name.'

'Yes,' I replied, 'and I'll certainly remember my first week.' I think I lost about two stone in sweat that day.

After some time I got my own conductor, Bob, who was a bit of a lad. We started to get to know how each of us worked and ended up getting on like a house on fire.

When we were 'dominoed out' (slang for full up) and he was upstairs collecting fares I used to see myself away from the stops instead of having him keep running up and down the bus to ring the bell. If it was quiet he would sometimes sit upstairs in the front and have a smoke; he would look down the bus to the mirror by the stairs and stamp his feet if the platform was clear, but when he did this dust use to spill down on me, so I had to tell him not to do it any more.

One day we were sailing along and I presumed Bob was having a smoke upstairs. It was a very quiet day, passengers were getting on and off and I was happy. That was until a passenger came up to the nearside window and said, 'Driver, do you know you haven't got a conductor?' I looked confused and then he told me that he had seen my conductor hop off the bus a few stops ago. Just as I began to get annoyed my conductor suddenly came up on the bus behind, 'Where have you been?' I asked.

'I jumped off to get a paper.'

'I'm not a mind reader,' I said angrily, 'I didn't know you were getting off.'

We were on the early turn one week when we discovered that there was a man who would always wait at the garage exit to jump on to the first bus of the day out of the depot. We had not known this before, so on our first morning on this shift he got on and offered Bob a £5 note for his fare. Bob explained that we were just starting and he did not have enough change, so he allowed the man a free ride to work.

This happened all week until Friday when Bob said, 'He's in for a shock today!' The man got on as usual and offered Bob the fiver and Bob smiled and gave him his change in coins. I think he got the message and from then on he always had the right fare. There was always someone trying it on.

After leaving Canning Town we had to go to Woolwich and then run back to the depot, so I would give the old bus some stick along the Silvertown Way, a nice wide road where you could give it some welly. I was sailing along so that I could get more time on the stand, when I looked up to see that my power indicator light had gone out in the cab, meaning that I had lost power, and on looking through the windscreen I saw that the wiring was waving about and hanging down. Bob stood under the stairs looking through the bus as he always did, thinking I was a crazy bugger. I came to a stop and got out, which Bob had a go at me for. 'You daft idiot, all we had to do was go to Woolwich and run in, now we're stuck here.' It stopped all the buses on our section, so we got in touch with the depot, though it never took them long to realise there was a breakdown on a section.

The breakdown wrecker came out and one of the crew members asked angrily, 'What bloody speed were you doing to cause this amount of damage?' I answered that I was doing about thirty-five, but he grumbled, 'More like a hundred and five.' So we all sat there while they repaired the wiring. I had to go in and see the depot manager later and he told me to be more careful in future.

The early trolleybuses were not all that fast, their top speed was probably about thirty-five miles per hour, but with a full load (about seventy-five people) you were lucky to get twenty-five mph. You had to stand up to steer round corners (there was no power steering of course). The later buses could manage about forty-five miles per hour, but if you were running late and you couldn't get any more speed, there was nothing you could do to keep to time. They were also almost completely silent; you could be saying goodbye to someone and when you looked round the bus was gone.

I pulled up at Upton Park once and saw a man pushing his wheelbarrow full of fruit and vegetables over the station hill. I pulled away from the stop and as I did so the man suddenly turned his barrow out to go past a parked car. Because the buses were so silent he was unaware of me and hit the side of the bus so that he and his barrow were tipped over and all his fruit and vegetables ran down the hill. The passengers on the bus started calling out that I was a madman. Even though it wasn't my fault Bob suggested I go down to the Boleyn and tell the inspector, and he would get all of the details; so I went to the depot and filled out an accident report.

On 6 March 1939, at 6.45 am, the first female Mayor of West Ham became the first person to be issued with a ticket for the new trolleybus which had come in to replace the trams. Her name was Daisy Parsons and she was an ex-suffragette; a plaque was erected in her name in the bus afterwards.

I had this bus one evening and nearly managed to blow it up. There were blinds to pull down behind the driver to stop the interior lights reflecting on the windscreen, and on this particular evening I had one behind me down and the nearside one up so that the conductor could come up to talk.

With the bus going flat out I over-ran the motor and knocked my main switches out. There was a bang and an almighty flash which lit the cab up like daylight. Bob said afterwards that you had never seen anyone move so fast as the lady and her daughter who were right behind me in the front seats, as they looked to see if I was all right. Bob told them not to worry about me, 'He's always sodding about. I don't take any notice, I've got used to him now,' he said.

I used to play a few jokes on Bob to pass the time. When we were on late shifts and it was relatively quiet, I would pull up at a stop and watch Bob through the interior mirror. He would go to the end of the platform and look around to see what I had stopped for. Drivers would often pull in to a stop to kill time if they ran early at night. We would sit there for a few moments and then he would ring the bell, but I would muffle it with my hands. I used to watch him pressing, and through my hand I would feel the tick, tick, tick, and I would just sit there; eventually he would walk through the bus and shout that the bell wasn't working.

'Why? Have you rung it?' I would ask.

'Yes, but I couldn't hear it,' he would reply.

So I would say, 'Well, ring it now,' and when he pulled the bell cord I would let it ring. 'That's working all right,' I would say, and away we would go to the next stop and I would repeat the joke again.

He said, 'I'm bloody sure that bell isn't working properly, I think we'll have to run the bus into the depot.'

Often, when we would go past a bus stop the bell would ring and you would wonder if they wanted that stop or the next one. So I would pull up and look round at the passenger who in turn would look round to see why I had pulled up and would then look guilty. I would have to shout, 'Did you want this stop?' and the passenger would say no, the next one. It would happen sometimes that passengers did want the first stop, but they were a little bit slow.

One day I was going down to the Crooked Billet and all the factory workers were standing on the back waiting to get off. I knew they wanted to get off at the factory gates, but I thought, 'If they don't ring the bell I'm taking them to the next stop.' Nobody rang so I went flying by and then they really thought about ringing: 'Ding, ding, ding,' but it was too late. When I stopped at the next stop I thought they were going to lynch me, but I said, 'What do you think I am, a mind reader? I don't know where you want to get off, you should ring the bell.'

Later in the week on the same duty we were going from the Crooked Billet to Woolwich, and as we were approaching the Billet I met the bus in front of us going the opposite way. By rights he should have waited until we pulled on the stand and left, which meant that there would be five minutes between buses, but his leaving early now made us eight minutes apart. I told Bob and he told me to wait and see what happened tomorrow; this bus was from the Walthamstow garage, our opposition.

The next day and the next the same thing happened, which meant that we were picking up passengers that were meant for him and Bob was working harder. Although he did not complain, I did, and I started 'dragging the road' (slang for going slow). In no time at all I had buses queuing up behind me (they could not go anywhere because of the trolleys) and the inspectors were phoning ahead to inform others that I was dragging the road and had disrupted the bus service.

When I got to the Boleyn the inspector asked me what had happened, saying that it wasn't like me to act like this. So I explained the tricks that this other crew was pulling on us; he told me to turn in at Canning Town for a cup of tea and a cool down.

So we parked the bus on a bus turning circle, pulled the trolleys down and went into the café for a cup of tea to settle the nerves. The next day they put an inspector at the Billet.

I once pulled up on the Crooked Billet bus stand when the bus in front had a black driver. As he went to pull away on to the roundabout a lorry driver had words with him about his pulling out. This started to become racially abusive and, in a fit of temper, the bus was driven straight across the road so that it collided with the lorry, taking much of its side and the windows out. Of course the bus was then defective, so once again we had a double road.

When we were on the 685 route, which was Crooked Billet to North Woolwich, we used to meet up with the number 40 diesel bus running from Wanstead to Camberwell Green. When we got to Wanstead Flats we would stop and use the pub toilets so that the number 40 would go in front and pick all the passengers up, giving us a free ride. However, they soon cottoned on to this and hung about, making us run late; it was war. Eventually they used to stop and hide from us. Talk about cat and mouse! We would do anything to give the conductor an easy life.

Pat and I bought a Ford Popular. I took all the wheels off and under-coated all the wings and as much of the underside as I could. It looked a picture and is probably still running today. I know it will certainly never rust.

I had been on the buses for about a year and a half and was quite settled in my ways. When I was on the early turn I would be ready for bed early, seeing as I was up at four in the morning. I would say to Pat, 'Are you coming to bed?'

'No, go in and I'll be in later.'

I was starting to get the impression that she wanted to get rid of me, though I didn't know why, so I went to bed and lay there thinking. I suspected that she was writing to someone, although why I thought that at the time I will never know. The next morning I got up at four o'clock and looked in her bag, and there was an unaddressed envelope inside.

'I can read that letter, put it in another envelope and she will never know,' I thought. The letter was to a man (I later found out he was a foreman at her firm), telling him that she loved him and couldn't wait to get me out, so that he could move in to our flat – our home. I went into the bedroom and said, 'I've found your letter.'

She just looked up and said, 'Well, now I don't have to tell you.'

I walked out and went to work. This letter also said that my mother- and father-in-law agreed with the situation. I don't know how I drove the bus that day. Bob was worried for me. Although I hadn't told him anything, he knew something was wrong. Also, I kept passing my father-in-law going in the opposite direction and he couldn't understand why I was ignoring him.

When I had finished my duty I went back to the depot where my father-in-law was waiting for me, wanting to know what had been going on all morning. So, I gave him the letter, saying 'You are a part of this.'

He flatly denied this and said, 'Yes, I know this fellow is coming round, but it is to see my other daughter, Linda.' It turned out that my mother-in-law knew that he was in fact seeing Pat while my father-in-law and I were at work.

I went back to my parents' house and they were quite shocked. My father was not one to mix his words and he said, 'In that case, you are well rid of her.'

I got my sister's husband and some of my friends and we went round and took everything out of the flat; what I could not give away we smashed. My father-in-law said,

'You've not left her anything, you've even taken the nails out of the door.'

I said, 'If he wants to live with her, let him buy her a home, he's not having mine.'

We had been married for five years when we parted. Fortunately there had been no children.

Chapter 6

Seasonal Coach Work

MY father was still driving for Towler's, but he also did some coach driving part-time at the weekends for Essex County Coaches, which mainly involved touring. He told me, 'I will see the manager of the coaches and see if he can give you a job,' and made arrangements for me to have an interview.

I went to see the manager, Joe Waterhouse, who told me that I was to apply for a PSV (Public Service Vehicle) licence. The driver's licence for trolleybuses was totally different from petrol buses as, apparently, trolleybuses came under light railways. He said that he already had two more drivers going for their test, so we could all go together. In the meantime, whenever I had time to spare I could go to the garage and have some tuition on driving the coaches with one of the regular drivers.

I met up with Wally Couch, the senior driver, who used to take me out to get to know the coaches: AEC Reliances with Roe bodies. We would drive all round the Wanstead flats and then practise reversing.

The day came for our tests, so I met up with the two drivers at the garage. One of them looked like Arthur Askey, the comedian. He apparently already had a PSV, but only for 29-seater coaches, so he wanted an upgrade to all types of single deckers.

The other driver asked me if I felt confident, to which I answered, 'Yes.' He then informed me that this was his fourth time, to which I replied, 'Well, I'm not confident now!'

We had to report to the Lambeth carriage office. The examiner came out and said he would take the driver with the licence first, and so off we went, all around the West End of London. When it was my turn we went all round Victoria too. Finally it was the third driver's go and he made a right hash of it; we were up and down kerbs as he crashed through the gears. Wally, the regular driver, kept looking round at us sitting in the back, pulling faces of disgust at the antics of this driver, but to keep the examiner's attention he kept talking to him about the tours.

We arrived back at the carriage office and drove into the courtyard and were then told to put the off-side front wheel on a mark painted on the ground, and then reverse the coach back up to the wall without knocking it down, which we each did in turn. The examiner turned to us and said, 'Right, boys, come and get your badges.' We had passed.

When we went in to see the manager he said to us, 'Boys, I want you to go away and get a job on Grey-Green's Coaches, and after you have got some coaching experience you can come back here and I will let you drive my coaches.'

That evening my father came home and told me that I was to see the coach manager for a job. I explained to him what the manager had said, but he replied, 'I know, he did not want the other two, so he told you all to get some experience first. But you have a job.' I had to wait until the summer season began at the beginning of April before I could hand my notice in to London Transport. I was twenty-six by then.

I explained to Bob what had happened with Pat and that I was leaving and he wished me well, saying that he had enjoyed our working together and would miss me.

I reported to the coach garage on the Monday morning and met all the drivers for the coming season as well as those who had stayed on through the winter months. The ones who had stayed on were veteran drivers who knew all you could know about English history. The manager used to say, 'There are coach drivers and then there are the gentlemen of Essex County Coaches.'

He sent six of us seasonal drivers with the service van to Duple Motor Bodies to collect five new Bedford coaches. When we got back to the garage the manager asked me what I thought of the coaches. I thought it was a bit strange of him to ask me, with all the more experienced drivers about, so I told him, 'Yes, they were good.'

'Excellent,' he said. 'One of them is yours, so look after it.'

These coaches were basically for beanos (the beach trips) and private parties; the main touring coaches were AEC Reliances. I started doing local tours to Windsor and Stratford-upon-Avon, Anne Hathaway's cottage, Warwick, Hampton Court, London, the galleries and trips to the coast and theatres. One day the manager called me in to the office and said, 'I want you to take over the Irish tour.' This was not as good as it may sound. It was basically an eleven-day tour to Ireland, but my part only involved four days of travel: two days to Holyhead, North Wales and two days back to London after the passengers had had their seven days in Ireland.

So I lost my new Bedford to take over the AEC

Reliance. The driver who normally did this trip was going on a seven-day tour so the manager thought that it would be a good start for me. The driver did come on the first trip with me, however, to show me the way and the stops.

We left on Monday, picking up our passengers at Kings Cross coach station and making our way out of West London for our first coffee stop at Amersham, to Banbury and its Cross for lunch and then to Warwick for sight-seeing and tea. On leaving Warwick we turned off past the race course to Kidderminster, going past the carpet factories, then on to the Long Mynd hotel in Church Stretton, close to the local cemetery. I joked with my passengers that you could not get lost, as we were in the dead centre of town.

Tuesday took us out through Shrewsbury and Oswestry to Llangollen for coffee, on to Betws-y-Coed for lunch and the sights of Swallow Falls, then on to Bangor for tea and across the Menai Bridge. We then went on to the Isle of Anglesey, the largest Welsh island, with a short stop at Llanfairpwllgwyngyllgogerychwyrndrobwllllantysiliogogo-goch, the station with the longest name (fifty-eight letters and nineteen syllables), finishing at the County Hotel at Holyhead.

I became friendly with a local in the hotel bar that evening and got him to write out the long name in its syllables and pronounce them slowly until I was quite fluent in my pronunciation. It used to give the passengers a kick when I said the name.

We had an evening meal in the hotel and then we would run the passengers down to the ferry at about eight o'clock in the evening and put them safely on board the night ferry to Dún Laoghaire in Southern Ireland.

As it was the first trip there was nobody to bring home,

but if there were any returning passengers we would go down to the dock on Wednesday morning and pick them up, making our way to Conway for morning coffee. We would drive through St Asaph, with its beautiful white cathedral, one of the smallest in the kingdom, and then down the Horse Shoe pass, across the River Dee to Llangollen for lunch and on to Shrewsbury for tea. We would head back to the Long Mynd hotel in Church Stretton for an over-night stop.

On Thursday we would go to Cleobury Mortimer for coffee at a small antiques café I had found, and to vary the tour a bit we stopped at Stratford-upon-Avon for lunch, visiting Anne Hathaway's cottage. We headed on to Beaconsfield for afternoon tea and then back to Kings Cross and home. That would be my job four days a week, then I would get Fridays off, coming back Saturday and Sunday to do the day-trips, and heading off again on Monday.

I carried on doing this over the summer months, during which time I met many interesting people. On one trip I was standing by the coach in Llangollen when one of my passengers approached me and started making small talk. The conversation worked its way round to the coach and he ask me if I had ever been caught speeding. I replied, 'No, I keep my eyes open and normally you can smell them,' which, looking back now, must have sounded a bit cocky.

'We can catch you any time of the day,' he replied.

'Why? Who are you?'

'I am the Chief Constable of the Wiltshire Constabulary.' He then went on to ask me what my maximum speed was (I thought to myself, 'Well, I'm not telling you'). 'Fifty-five miles per hour,' I said.

'No way. I have a stop watch with me and I have been timing you between telegraph poles. I calculate that your maximum speed is around sixty-five.'

'This is his holiday,' I thought. 'Don't they ever rest?'

Later in the day when I started to pull out of the car park a brewery lorry was delivering to the pub and the traffic became jammed up. The next thing I knew the door of the coach had opened and this Chief Constable had got out and started directing traffic. When I spoke to the passengers later they said, 'He's been like this all the holiday.'

I was trying to make a bit of time up and further along the road I came up behind a car with two young lads in it who were plodding along quite merrily at about thirty miles per hour. The road soon became clear enough for me to overtake, so I hooted to let them know I was going to pass them. As I got alongside them they looked up at me and started laughing and racing me; I then had no option but to drop back behind them.

I made three attempts to pass the car and each time they started laughing and racing me. I thought, 'Oh, they want to play.' So when the road became clear again I made another attempt to pass them and again they started racing me, but this time I was coming through and as I got alongside them I watched them in the near-side mirror and gradually started to ease the coach in. I could see they were not laughing now, only panicking, so I made it through. I would never have got close enough to cause an accident, but the sides of the coach were big enough to frighten them.

When we had our next stop the Chief Constable came up to me and said, 'I suppose you thought you were clever doing that.'

I said, 'No, but if they want to play games, I'm the kiddie to play with.'

On another trip something had upset me and I was ranting on to the passengers sitting beside me about the police and they kept laughing. I thought that it was me they were laughing at, which made me even madder. As we made our way through Wales I finally asked, 'What are you laughing at?'

'If you knew who we were you would laugh,' they replied.

'Why? Who are you?'

'Magistrates.'

'That's all I need,' I thought. On the way home they asked if I would drop them off at Uxbridge. I hesitated: 'Well, it's a bit dodgy for parking around by the station.'

'Don't worry,' they assured me. 'If you get caught and come up before us we'll see you all right.'

'I bet you would,' I thought.

On another trip I had a man and his wife sitting beside me and the man kept asking me about Wilson gear boxes, what I thought of pre-selector gear boxes and whether they would be man enough for long-distance work. I said, 'Are you anything to do with AEC vehicles?'

He said, 'No, I am a London Transport driving examiner.'

'That's all I need, you sitting beside me!' I relied, making him laugh. 'I hope you aren't like the other passenger I had,' and I told him about the police chief.

'You had every right to go to the nearest police station and have him taken off the coach for harassing you when driving a PSV vehicle,' he said.

'I couldn't have done that,' I thought.

A few weeks after I had spoken to the police chief about speeding I was motoring along, when suddenly a motor cycle cop came up to my rear. They used to get right up close so that you could not see them behind you, so if someone was talking to you, or if you were distracted, you'd miss him approaching and then my heart would give a thump at the sight of him. He rode up along the side of the coach and I looked down at him, he put his hand out indicating me to lift my foot up, which I did, and then he sped off. I passed him further on along the road and he gave me the thumbs-up sign, and I gave a sigh of relief.

One weekend I was taking a day trip to Clacton and as usual we got held up by heavy traffic on the A12. It was a glorious day so I opened the front entrance door to let some air circulate, when a few yards in front I noticed a car on fire. The driver was running down the road asking anyone if they had a fire extinguisher. When he got to me he was looking down at the one by my feet so I could hardly say no. I unclipped it and gave it to him, not that it would have made much difference as the car was well alight, and then he gave me back the empty canister.

When I got back to the garage and told the manager what happened he had a right go and said, 'Did you get his name and address?'

'No,' I replied. 'He was more concerned with his car that was on fire.'

'Well, who is paying for it to be replaced? You left the coach with no extinguisher. Suppose the coach had a fire!'

'So much for good will,' I thought.

The summer season finished and the autumn tours began. I was in the garage one day and the manager called me into the office and said, 'You're going away on Monday'.

'Where to?'

'Scotland!'

I panicked: 'I've never been to Scotland.'

'Well, now is the time to learn all about it and don't worry, just map your tour out day by day. Anyway, you'll be following other coaches and they will keep an eye on you.' I thought to myself, 'It's all right if you're on your own, but with fifty-one passengers it's a different thing.'

On Monday I went to Kings Cross coach station and pulled into the stand to start loading passengers. One of the regular drivers came up to me and said, 'Take your PSV badge off and put it in your pocket, touring drivers don't show their badges.' From then on I never wore my badge until later when I returned to the buses and was pulled up by an inspector for not wearing it.

Most of the coaches going to Scotland went up the Archway Road on to the North Circular. We stopped at Baldock for coffee, Stamford for lunch, and Doncaster (with its Gaumont cinema) for tea, before reaching Harrogate, Leeds or Wakefield where we had our overnight stop.

My first night's stop was at Buxton. We went through Oakham, Melton Mowbray, across to Derby, through Bakewell and to Buxton.

The second night was to be at Dumfries. We headed out through Macclesfield, over the Cat and Fiddle Road, passing places such as Knutsford, Penrith and Carlisle. On my way up if I thought there was something of interest I would ask the passengers if they wanted to stop and of course they would always say yes; I don't think they had ever been on a tour with so many stops.

The worst part was that after you let them out you had to round them all up again; it always brought out the cowboy in me. I should have been at the County Hotel at Dumfries for our six o'clock evening meal, but because of all the extra stops I was still in Carlisle at six o'clock. I had to make an excuse, so I stopped and phoned the hotel to say I had got a puncture and that I was running late. 'Don't worry,' they said. I told the passengers to back my story and I drove like a bat out of hell.

In the evening I had a phone call from Charlie Howard, a senior driver, to see if I was all right. I told him what had happened and he said, 'You don't have time to make stops other than the ones printed on your tour brochure.'

Each night I sat in my room looking at my maps and planning my next day, after which I had a walk round the town to see which way to leave. I was learning slowly. We left Dumfries in the morning, heading north to Ayr for the Station Hotel at the mouth of the River Ayr, Robert Burns country, where they had the afternoon free.

From Ayr we travelled along the coast through to Balloch, on the shores of Loch Lomond, for lunch. We would get a boat ride on the loch (half a crown for all the riders).

We would leave Balloch and travel on to Aberfoyle in the Trossachs (the bristly country), to Loch Katrine and Callander for tea and to look at the woollen mills. All of this activity was good because at the end of the season we received a percentage of what the passengers had spent on their trips.

We then made our way to Edinburgh where we would stop for two nights and have an extensive tour on the fifth day. Charlie Howard introduced me to the castle guides; you could give them a tip and they would take your passengers on a guided tour of the castle which they always liked, as they could go shopping down the Royal Mile to the Palace of Holyroodhouse.

That evening Charlie phoned me and said, 'In the morning come round to my hotel and you can follow me to Jedburgh where we stop for coffee, but I will leave you there because I will have to derv up, and you will probably catch me up anyway.'

The next day I left Jedburgh and began making my way to Newcastle upon Tyne for our lunch stop. Further along the road I caught up with a lorry carrying a load of steel girders travelling quite slowly, which kindly pulled over as far as he dared to allow me to pass. However, when we got to Carter Bar, with its 1,371 feet height, the passengers wanted to get out to take photos of the border signs. When I looked up after this, the lorry had passed us again and I thought 'Oh no, I've got to go through getting past him again.' We boarded the coach and made our way along the road, catching up with the lorry. Once again he pulled over while still moving and I started to overtake him.

However, I suddenly realised that the steering was being pulled away from my hands towards a deep ditch which the coach started to veer into. 'I mustn't brake,' I thought, 'because a sudden stop will make the coach fall on its side.'

So I just let it run until it stopped on its own, dropping into the ditch and resting on a dry wall on the other side. The side windows and panels were torn out until the coach finally hit a telegraph pole which smashed the windscreen and stopped it altogether.

All this happened at about ten miles per hour. There was panic on the coach and I had blood pouring down the right side of my face. I had no idea what had hit me, but my main concern was the passengers, so I scrambled out through the shattered windscreen and climbed up the bank for help. It's amazing where doctors and helpful people come from; they seemed to emerge from nowhere and scrambled to the coach, managing to get the passengers out to sit on the road side. They phoned for ambulances from Newcastle Infirmary, but as they were so far away we were told that the Army ambulances from the nearby Otterburn barracks would be coming. The local bus was then stopped to take the walking wounded to the hotel down the road.

The Army ambulances arrived, but one of them managed to rip the side of the local bus as it passed it, and so the bus driver was jumping up and down in anger. It looked like a scrap yard; there were metal panels all over the place, but at last we were ferried to the infirmary. I kept asking people if the police wanted to see me, but I was told not to worry and that they would see me in good time. The hospital wanted me to stay in overnight but I just wanted to get home, so they discharged me and took me to the station by taxi and put me on the train for London.

Thankfully nobody was seriously hurt, only very shocked. Charlie, whom I had been following, started making enquiries about what had happened to me when I didn't join him in Newcastle. Once he heard that a coach had gone into a ditch he notified the garage and they got in touch with my parents; my father even came home from work.

I sat on the train reliving my past year; my wife had left me and now this had happened. When I got to London my father was waiting and his first words were: 'Did someone cut you up?'

'No', I said. My face was like a swollen football, I was still worrying about the police and why they had not contacted me yet.

After a few days I went down to the coach garage to see Joe Waterhouse. He said to me, 'Get in that coach and go for a ride.'

'Where to?' I replied.

'I don't care. I don't want my star driver losing his confidence.'

'Well, I won't do that.' He insisted that I went for a ride, so I took the coach and drove round for half an hour and came back.

He looked at me carefully: 'You all right?'

'Yes,' I said.

A few weeks later I had to take my driving licence and insurance to Leytonstone police station. The police sergeant said, 'We have a letter here from the Roxburghshire police asking for you to make a statement. It would be in your own interest to make a statement otherwise they might start probing.'

I said, 'Well, I have nothing to hide,' and proceeded to write out what had happened. I also added that I thought the camber on the road was too great and that the road was not wide enough for two heavy vehicles to pass each other.

I later received a letter from the Roxburghshire police saying that no action was being taken against me and that my suggestions were being taken up by the local council; road improvements had in fact been in force already, but due to the heavy rainfall the road had subsided under the weight of the coach. When I travelled over the road later it was much wider and the camber not so great. Also a new telegraph pole had been added; it was a much better road.

Chapter 7

Aero Petroleum

THE season was at an end and that meant I had to look for another job. Luckily, one of the ex-coach drivers who now worked for a private oil company, Aero Petroleum, called in to the coach garage one day and told the manager that his boss wanted five drivers for the winter season and the manager elected me as one of those to go for an interview. The five of us arrived and were taken in. The boss said, 'I suppose you are all 'artic' drivers?'

The driver I had relieved on the Irish tour said, 'We will drive anything you have here, guv.'

I thought, 'Here we go again.' I and two of the others said we were not artic drivers, so the boss said, 'Well, I really need artic drivers, but I will get the foreman fitter to take you for a test.' We all went out on a test in a BMC artic; on my turn I took us all round Barking and then on coming back to the yard I was told to back it in between two tankers. I could have got it in sideways there was that much room, so he informed the boss that we had all passed and we were given a starting date.

The fleet of vehicles the company had were AEC Mammoth Majors, Atkinson eight-wheelers, Bullnose Austin four-wheel tankers, and BMC (British Motor Company) rigids and artics. The BMCs were glorified forward-control Austins with the engine in the cab; it was so light that when it was fully loaded the front used to lift up. They also had the Scammell trailer coupling.

I was placed with the driver Charlie Lawrence on one of the two Atkinsons on heavy fuel oil (the second was only used in the winter season). Over breakfast at the Broadview café one of the BMC artic drivers told us about his experience with another of the coach drivers. He told us that they were going up Blackheath hill (before the road layout of today) to get on the A2, but the motor was struggling. The coach driver was in second gear and kept looking at the tanker driver for instructions. 'We had practically come to a standstill,' the tanker driver said.

He described how the coach driver pushed the gear lever into first and took his foot off the clutch so that the motor reared up. 'I leapt out fully expecting to see the trailer going back down the hill,' he said. 'I called him everything under the sun and told him to get out of the cab and would not let him drive again. I will never ride on his coach.' In fact, he never went out with that coach driver again. The tanker drivers all said, 'We thought coach drivers were the elite, but we have a different opinion now.'

Charlie and I got on well and I loved driving the motor, even though it was flat out at thirty-five miles per hour. We were carrying heavy fuel oil, so Charlie showed me how to load at the oil terminal, pump off at the deliveries using the cargo pump and always to make sure to open the delivery valve, otherwise you would have a burst hose. The oil was loaded hot because it was so thick that it would not run otherwise. The tank was lagged to keep the heat in; if you did have a spillage you had to bring a shovel because it went like tar once it was cold.

I had been with Charlie a few days when I was called in to the office and told that on Monday I was to take over a new BMC unit coming home and was to connect a trailer in the yard. I protested and said, 'But I am not an artic driver, surely you have me mixed up with one of the drivers who said that they were?' I was then told that out of the five drivers I was the one recommended as best to drive the artic.

I pleaded with Charlie to help me and he said, 'Look at it this way, you will have a new motor and the others will get the old ones.' So that was that – I was on my own again.

Monday came and I connected up to the heavy fuel oil tank, following Charlie to the Shell terminal at Thames Haven, to load up with black oil. I then followed him up Red Lion Hill to the Broadview café for breakfast, our morning ritual, and sometimes we even met up in the afternoon for tea. I thought, 'I could enjoy this job.'

The coach firm always arranged to take all the staff out for an end-of-season treat, and this time we were taken to the theatre. On the way there I spoke to one of the drivers who had been with me at the oil company and we discussed our deliveries for the next day. He said that he never waited for the boilerman to arrive and would pump the load in and sign the delivery ticket himself, but I said that I always waited for him so that I knew everything was OK before I started delivering.

I arrived at the block of flats the next morning and went to the boilerman's station. He wasn't there so I waited and looked suspiciously at my delivery instructions. When he eventually arrived I said, 'Before we start, will you see if a delivery has already been made as I was talking to my mate last night and I'm sure he said he had this delivery also.'

'Is that the one who has always delivered and gone before I get here?' the boilerman replied.

'Yes.'

'The times I have told him to wait for me,' he grumbled. So I followed the boilerman downstairs to the tanks and he opened the trap door and exclaimed, 'Oh, he has been here all right, the load is all on the ground!' I notified the office and they had to send another tanker to pump out as much as they could and the rest had to be sanded and shoveled up.

Another time I had to deliver to a pharmacy in Kings Cross; I pulled up and went inside and the security man said, 'Just outside the office on the wall you will find a trap door, open it with this key and you will find the oil connection pipe.' So I went out and connected up and came back inside. 'Where are the tanks?' I asked.

'What do you want to know that for?'

'Well, I like to know where I am pumping to.'

'Don't worry, just pump the load in,' he finished. So I did.

I used to do this delivery quite often and would just go in and ask for the key to pump the load off. However, one day I was pumping merrily along and sitting in the cab when I heard screaming and shouting. When I looked up people were running about shouting, 'Switch it off! Switch it off!' By the time I knocked the cargo pump out and stopped pumping I think another two hundred gallons had disappeared into the factory. Apparently, when I arrived the security man should have sent down to the boilerman to tell him that a delivery was taking place and then the boilerman would direct the oil to whatever tank he wanted it to go to. This morning, however, he had forgotten to tell the boilerman so the oil was going into a tank which was already full.

After a while I was taken off the artic and given the

Atkinson eight-wheeler. I used to run with Charlie doing the nurseries all round Essex. After we had loaded at the Haven, Charlie would always insist that I went first so he could overtake me on Red Lion Hill (and I could flash him in) as his motor was just that bit faster than mine, but when we got to the Broadview café he would still let me buy the teas.

One morning when we were in the Broadview having finished our breakfast, one of Yiddle Davis's new Leyland eight-wheelers was blocking our exit. Charlie went back into the café to find the driver, who had just got his breakfast.

He told Charlie to move it if he could drive a decent lorry. I think he was joking, but Charlie went ahead and moved the lorry anyway. He said to the driver, 'What are those big holes round the foot pedals?' The driver explained that he had complained to the fitters that the pedals were scraping the floor panels when you pushed them down, so they got out the welding gear and made a big hole in the floor, telling him they would not scrape now and not to come in the workshop complaining. What an outfit! I heard many funny stories about Davis Transport.

On the subject of awkward parking, I used to deliver to a block of flats half-way up Highgate Hill where I would have to pull up and run across the road to find the boilerman so that he could try and find out if anybody wanted to get their cars out before I pulled in. It was a very tight place to get in; the second-floor balcony just missed the oval of the tank so you had to be very careful in case you punctured it. The boilerman told me that all was well so I pulled in, connected up and started pumping.

A short time later a lady came up to me and said, 'Move your vehicle. I want to get my car out.'

I explained that the boilerman had assured me that nobody wanted to come out and now that I was pumping I could not stop.

'I am not going to argue with you, get it out!'

The boilerman came over to me and said, 'I'm sorry, but you'll have to move.'

'Who the hell is she?' I asked.

The boilerman told me her name but it did not register with me: 'Who's that, then? A film star?'

'No,' he said. 'She's a Member of Parliament.' So I took my time, blew my lines, uncoupled the hoses, backed out across Highgate Hill, let her out and then came back in to finish the delivery. It turned out that she was Barbara Castle, who was a non-driver; she became Transport Secretary in 1965 and one of her claims to fame was the introduction of the Breathaliser. When she told me to let her car out, I saw it was chauffeur-driven.

I had a happier experience with another woman later in the season. On the side of the tank was written Aero, with a picture of a fighter plane. A young woman once came up to me and asked what I carried. I replied, 'Bubbles, for Aero chocolate.' She walked away very satisfied with my answer.

So it was not all bad; I did have a lot of successful deliveries over the winter seasons and I was with Aero Petroleum for a while.

One day I happened to get on a trolleybus and there was a new conductress under instruction and I thought, 'She's very nice.' In the evening I went round my mate John's house who was still on the buses, so I mentioned this conductress to him and he said, 'I will look out for her.'

A few nights later I went round to see him again (he was

very understanding and took pity on me as he knew Pat and all about my imminent divorce) and he said, 'I have something for you.' He gave me a piece of paper with an address on it. 'Remember telling me about that conductress?' he said, 'Well, I had tea with her and her driver on one of our breaks and told her about you and she said that if you want to take her out you will have to go round to her home and get her as she does not get picked up on street corners. I've made a date for you for seven o'clock on Saturday.

Her name is Anne.'

'You're joking,' I replied. 'She doesn't even know what I look like.'

On the Saturday when I pulled up outside her house and knocked on the door, it suddenly went through my mind: 'What if it's not the same girl?'

She opened the door: 'Hallo, you must be Al!'

I was lost for words and could only say, 'I didn't have time to wash the car.'

'In that case, we'll walk,' she said.

She lived in Custom House and one Saturday evening we had a ride out to Epping, stopping at a pub for a drink. On our way home we were going through the forest when suddenly a girl rushed out right in front of the car, waving her arms and shouting so that I had to swerve to miss her. I thought that she must either have been a nutter or just really wanted me to stop, but I was worried that if I did then someone would come out and rob us so I wanted to carry on, but Anne insisted I stopped. The girl jumped in the car and said that she had been in a club in the West End of London and a man had picked her up and brought her out here and attacked her. Her clothes were torn and she was very upset; she did not know where she was. Anne said, 'Don't worry; we will take you home to West London.' What could I say? I kept looking in the mirror expecting to see someone following us.

One evening Anne told me a funny story about her day at work. At Dames Road in Forest Gate there were some London Transport toilets for the bus men, so she told her driver to stop when he got there. She went in and locked the door but couldn't unlock it to get out. After some time the driver went in to find out why she was taking so long and she said, 'I can't get out!' So he tried, but he could not get the door open either.

The bus behind then arrived and so the driver took the trolleys down and transferred the people over, telling the driver to let the inspector know that she was locked in the toilet. She had to wait there until the maintenance crew came out to release her. 'I was in there for nearly two hours,' she said. Apart from being embarrassed she also had to take all the jokes from the bus crews.

She tried to convince me to return to the buses so that we could work together as a crew. I thought about it, but I declined. I enjoyed the coaches better than the buses. After a few more months of this the coach season began.

Little did I know that I would later be on the buses once more.

Chapter 8

Second Round of Coaches

AS soon as I arrived back at the coaches I was issued with polishes and window cleaning material and allocated an AEC Reliance with a Plaxton body, so cleaning became the order of the day. We needed to wash and polish away all the grime from the winter months before the summer tours started.

We had some new drivers start around that time; they were closer to my age than the regular elder drivers and we became known as the new boys on the job. As we were still learning to be tour drivers some of the elders got quite upset when they found out we were getting more beer money than them. This happened because the passengers did not want history pumped down their throats all the time which the older drivers were prone to do. We knew nothing, so had to learn as we went along. We joked around with the passengers and they seemed to like that better, and of course personality played a big part.

As I left Kings Cross and entered the suburbs I would pull the microphone down and introduce myself, telling them my name was Alec, and that when I was born my parents could not agree on a name for me, until it was suggested I was named after my father's occupation. Then I would wait and someone would always call out, 'What was your father's occupation?'

I would say, 'Oh, he was an Alectrician.' It sounds corny now but it broke the ice. Then I would tell them I was their driver and courier for the length of whatever tour we were on, the stops we would make that day and any information I thought they should know.

I bought all the *Blue Guides* to Scotland, Wales and England and any other books I thought were good so that I could read up on the tour routes, and of course you always picked up the local information. However, before the summer season tours started we would fill in with spring and private tours. I was once given a private party of Russians to take about for a week, along with their guide and interpreter. I had to pick them up in a London hotel and take them on the usual trips to Stratford-upon-Avon, Hampton Court, Blenheim Palace, Warwick, Windsor and on the London tours.

Once when we were doing the London tour I pulled up in Trafalgar Square and they got out for a walkabout, so I told the interpreter that I would stay with the coach until I was moved. As I sat there a young lady and her son asked me in broken English to leave the coach and show them around. I tried to make her understand I could not leave the coach, so she asked if I could show her where Nelson was. I pointed to the top of the column. 'Oh!' she said, and pointed to her son to look up. 'What is that interpreter telling them?' I thought; she did not seem to have a clue.

The party then wanted to go to a typical English seaside town and Brighton was suggested. On the Sunday morning I picked them up and headed out of London. When we got on the A23 the interpreter came up to me and said, 'They would like to stop at one of your layabouts.'

'Our what?'

'Layabouts,' she repeated.

'You mean lay-by.'

'Oh, right,' she said.

I happened to stop at a lay-by where a Messerschmitt car was parked. It looked like a left-over fighter plane cockpit, with two small wheels on the front and a single wheel at the back, with a glass hood which lifted up on hinges to allow entry for the occupants who sat behind one another. They were all the rage at one time, as was the bubble car, so-named because it looked like a bubble, with the door entry in the front and the passengers sitting side by side. The Russians did not know what to make of this little machine and probably thought it was something like a Sputnik which had just dropped out of space. The people in the little car were having their sandwiches and wondered what the hell was happening, with all these people ranting away in a foreign language and leaning on their car to have their photos taken.

The next thing I knew they had put their gear away and shot off. The Russians were nearly getting knocked down trying to cross the dual carriageway and so I decided to continue to Brighton. In the late afternoon I returned home to the hotel; my job was done.

This was about the time that the Russians entered the Space Race and the Cold War. All the drivers who had taken the Russians about received little badges from them for this, and I collected some for services rendered.

We used to pick Russians up at the docks (I don't know where they had been) and take them to London hotels; we would always finish with a bottle of vodka and badges. I remember taking a party to Harlow to see the new town and its church with the steeple at the side rather than on the roof and thought jokingly, if anything starts, it's going to be Harlow that gets it.

The regular drivers stayed during the winter months to do odd jobs and general maintenance in the garage. One of these drivers was a lazy so and so, and always walked round with an empty bucket, wash leather, and a sponge; everybody knew him as a lazy b......

When I came back I missed him and asked where he was. I was told he was in hospital with a hernia and that they reckoned someone had filled his bucket with water when he wasn't looking.

The summer season was about to begin. It usually ran from about the beginning of May to September, with the autumn tours going until the end of October. I did a Lakes tour, with Kendal as its base, and a Cornwall spring tour, and then I got ready for the summer tours.

I started off doing my four-day section of the Irish tour and continued with it most of the way through the season. Towards the end of the season the manager of the County Hotel in Holyhead said that he had enjoyed my time at the hotel and that he could set his clock by me. I asked him what he meant and he said, 'Dead on six o'clock on a Tuesday night I look out my window and you're coming round the corner; you never fail.' Mind you, I used to give it some stick across Anglesey; I think they thought I was a low-flying aircraft stationed there.

I did a few autumn tours, including one to Scotland where I came to the scene of my previous accident; I was pleased to see that the road was wider and the camber straightened out. This area made me feel a bit uncomfortable, though; I wondered if I would ever meet up with any of the people who were on that tour with me.

On one of my weekends at home I was given a theatre trip to do. I picked the party up in the early evening and proceeded to the theatre where they were seeing *Starlight Express* and dropped them off. I was told to pick them up at 11.30 pm, so I made my way to Nine Elms, South London, to park up. I found a fish shop and sat in the coach enjoying my meal and listening to the radio. It then started pouring with rain. At 11 pm I started making my way back to the theatre and as I was approaching it I heard shouting and looked to see the organiser of my party trying to attract my attention. I stopped and he and his wife got in and said, 'Where have you been?'

'Why? You told me to pick you up at 11.30.'

'Yes, I know, but the roof of the theatre was leaking and the skaters were all falling over and having accidents so the show was cancelled.'

'Well, where is your party now?' I asked.

'Some have gone for a meal and some are making their own way home,' he replied. So you can go home on your own.' What a night.

I remember another theatre job where I was told by one of the senior drivers that after dropping off the party and parking up, if I made myself known to the theatre they would probably let me in. So I parked up and made my way back to the theatre. The manager said I could go in but I would have to stand at the back because all the seats were taken, and I said, 'Yes, that will be all right.'

I stood at the back of the theatre watching all these nuns singing and dancing and thought, 'I'm not really interested in religious plays,' so made for the exit. I later found out that it was *The Sound of Music*. Well, I didn't know! I was not told and I never even looked at the bill-board. What a fool I was.

I was on hire to Grey-Green Coaches one weekend and had to report to Mile End coach garage where I was given a Clacton and Walton service. I pulled in to a public house at Marks Tey near Chelmsford, the official stop for Grey-Green service coaches, and saw three London Transport double-deckers in the car park. The guv'nor of the pub was telling the drivers they could not stop there because there were too many people to cater for and anyway they only stopped there once in a blue moon and he had to cater for his regular service coaches; he made it very clear he did not want them to stop on their return journey either.

I pulled back into this pub on my journey back and these three buses were there again, only this time while trying to manoeuvre in the car park one of the buses had caught the overhanging roof of the pub. Apart from the damage to the upper deck of the bus it had also brought some of the pub's roof down. To say the least, the pub guv'nor was not a happy person that day.

When the season came to an end I returned to Aero Petroleum for another season delivering black oil. I was the only driver they had taken back out of the original five. This became my yearly routine: back and forth between the coaches and the tankers.

One episode I particularly remember from the tankers was when I was using a BMC artic, on gas and diesel oil, to deliver to a private house on an unadopted road which was full of pot holes.

I pulled up at this big house and started walking down the path where I was met by a lady walking towards me. She asked what I wanted, and I said, 'Heating oil delivery, Ma'am.'

She said, 'Oh, where is your vehicle?' So I pointed and she said, 'Well, leave it there, I don't want you on my drive.' Then she shouted to her son, 'Rodney! Get all those sacks from the garage!' She looked at me and said, 'I don't want any leaks from your couplings.' This was before hose reels.

I had to lay out ninety feet of one and a half inch hose made up of thirty-foot lengths. The son laid out the sacks across the lawns and paths and I had to put the hose in an open top tank. This was not a good idea, nowadays you have to have a proper fitting to the tank; trying to save money by not having one is definitely a bad idea.

When I was all set I started pumping and thought to myself that with the amount of work I have I will be here all day! So I opened the driver's door and got a piece of wood to jam the accelerator down and keep it at a fast tick-over (this was before hand throttles). The motor was revving up and shutting down as I tried to reach a happy medium. Once I was satisfied with the engine revs I looked up to see that the hose had come out of the tank and was swishing about quite merrily, shooting gas oil all up the side of the house and all over the garden; there was gas oil everywhere.

I didn't know what to do apart from shutting it all down. I then had to decide whether to leave the motor and start running or to face the lady. She then came running out, shouting, 'What the hell are you doing?'

Rather meekly I said, 'It came out.'

'I can bloody well see that,' she said. I gathered my gear up and left; the insurance would settle all of it.

One of the drivers who came with me to Aero was Reg, a big fellow and strong as a lion. We went down to Thames Haven near Stanford-le-Hope (we picked up all our loads from Shell) and made arrangements to meet at the Broadview café for breakfast.

I was loaded first and got to the café and ordered my breakfast. Reg was driving one of the two Dennis Pax artics Aero had. As I was sitting there I heard an almighty crash, bang, wallop, and looked out the window to see what all the noise was, but couldn't find anything. The next thing I knew, Reg came in with two men holding him up. 'What happened?' I asked.

The two men said, 'Give him a cup of tea quick. Go and look at the waggon.'

I walked outside and saw that it was in bits: radiator, mudguards and bonnet, all scattered over the car park. It seemed that Reg had come into the car park so fast that he had hit a pot hole and shot up, hitting his head on the roof of the cab and nearly knocking himself out. I couldn't stop laughing. He said it had felt like hitting a brick wall.

He phoned the depot and they towed the motor back for repair. However, this took a few weeks and by that time they had forgotten that the load would have gone hard, so when they told him to recouple the tank he hit it so hard that it all fell apart again. The funny thing is he was a very experienced tanker driver, having driven for the firm Crow Carrying.

The depot had the tank taken away to be steam heated. Inside the fuel oil tanks there were steam pipes, so steam could be put through the tanks to thaw the oil and make it slightly thinner. Sometimes when you started to pump, if it had not been used for a few days, the pump would give out a thumping noise until the warm oil circulated.

Another of Reg's incidents occurred after someone had upset him in the office. He jumped into the lorry, grasped the steering wheel and started wrenching it in a temper, until the steering wheel broke in half. He gasped,

'Whoops!' and went back to the office with the two halves and said, 'I've broken the steering wheel.'

They said, 'How can you break a steering wheel?' He knew how.

There was another driver who had come from Crow Carrying and he drove the other Dennis Pax which was a gate change gearbox. The other drivers used to say, 'He thinks he is the only driver who can drive it because Crows had gate change Scammels; we don't want to drive the old rust bucket anyway.'

They had an ex-coach driver at Aero who wore an old coach driver's hat with badges on it and drove a small Austin 500-gallon tanker with two 250-gallon compartments. They kept him mainly on petrol, but if he had diesel, paraffin or gas oil, it had to be pumped off with the small hand pump at the back which you had to move from side to side and took ages. He would always have to have a mate to help him if this happened.

The guv'nor told him that they were getting him a new chassis and they would get a cargo pump fitted so that he did not have to keep using the hand pump. But he said, 'No, I don't want a cargo pump.'

The guv'nor said, 'But you will have to carry on with the hand pump.'

'That's all right,' he said. After the guv'nor had gone he told us, 'I am no fool; they will keep me on petrol now.'

Of course, if someone else had the motor now and they had to use the hand pump they would always insist on a mate too. When I sometimes had this vehicle I would get embarrassed, because when other drivers pulled up at your side you had to look up at them; they would always call you 'little squirt', because when you were on the loading racks you had a job to reach the loading arm.

It was nearing the end of March and work was easing up, so I started getting ready to swap jobs from the hard winter life to the summer holidays. It was time to go back to the coaches.

When I arrived back there I was promoted, with one of the younger drivers, to the nine- and twelve-day tours of Scotland. His name was Ian and we became good mates. We began with a couple of spring tours in Devon and Cornwall, which mostly involved having a central base at a hotel with trips out on various days.

Then we started the summer tours. I began with the nine-day one and Ian the twelve and then we would change over. We took over two AEC Reliances with Duple Britannia bodies. We would leave on the Saturday for the nine-day tour and once it was over we would have one night at home, leaving again on Monday morning for the twelve-day, and coming home on the Friday week; this went on for all the summer season.

On our first day we would head for Lancaster, going through places such as Dunstable, Newcastle-under-Lyme, Wigan and Lancaster on the River Lune. On Sunday we would make our way to Newby Bridge and Lake Windermere. We then headed over the Kirkstone Pass (1,489 ft above sea level) and along Lake Ullswater. We would then move on to Penrith, Carlisle, Gretna Green, stopping for the mock marriage at the Old Blacksmith's Forge, and then to Annan in Dumfries.

After leaving Dumfries we went through a small village named Hollywood, so I told the passengers to look out for any film stars that might be about getting their shopping. We would then drive to Gourock, where we boarded the ferry across to Dunoon, so I would have to back the coach across the ferry deck from side to side, not like the modern roll-on/roll-off, so that they could get two coaches next to each other.

When I arrived at the hotel and had settled the passengers I started to unload the cases. I could see the waitresses looking out of the window to see what the driver was like. All the hotels would have different coach companies stopping there during the season, and you would get one waitress taking a liking to a particular driver and then always making a fuss of him when he arrived. There was plenty of opposition in Dunoon because the American Navy was there, but when my turn came I blew it.

I came down for dinner and was shown to a table where a young waitress, Vi, hung round and fussed over me, running for my every whim. I, however, had taken rather a shine to another of the waitresses serving my passengers. I said to Vi, 'See that waitress over there?'

She looked across at where I was pointing and said, 'Who, Morag?'

'Yes, well, I just heard her say to my passengers that you had more time to chat because you did not have as many tables to wait on as she had.'

I have never seen anybody move so fast! The next thing I knew they were both arguing and pointing to me. I had blown it. I had only meant it as a joke, but from then on I was on my own and I had to serve myself, although I did redeem myself later.

We would stay in Dunoon for three days, giving me a few days off. One time I was staying there I bought a newspaper to read all about the Great Train Robbery.

Thursday was a long day; we travelled our way round Holy Loch, Loch Eck and Loch Fyne to Inveraray and Tyndrum. We passed the Bridge of Orchy, Loch Tulla,

Loch Ba and Glen Coe. We would then go along Loch Linnhe to Fort William and along Loch Lochy to Fort Augustus. Our destination was the Columba Hotel at Inverness, but because we were often running late we had to have dinner in the hotel at Fort Augustus.

However, I would always arrive there too early, so I would take the passengers to the Monastery to see the monks and their little gift shop. The monks used to look forward to my visits and I got on very well with the Abbot.

After our dinner at Fort Augustus we made for Inverness. I drove like a bat out of hell around the bends along Loch Ness to try and make up time. It was in the dark with the headlights full on so I could see if anything was coming the other way. I never thought for a minute about the passengers until I pulled up outside the Columba Hotel at eight-thirty and they got out and said, 'What a ride!' Their adrenalin had been flowing with the excitement (or maybe it was fright); but I had just wanted to get finished as I was knackered. They said that it had felt as though they were on a rally and that it was the best part of the tour.

Driving round the lochs took all your concentration, especially in the very narrow places and tight bends. Much later, when I had retired, we travelled the same roads in our camper and found that they had been moved away from the loch side and were much better. I was glad as I had never been happy driving along the side of Loch Lomond, with nothing separating you from it; I'm sure there must have been a few mishaps with cars.

On Friday we would go straight down the A7 to Edinburgh.

We would leave Edinburgh on Saturday and head to Jedburgh on the River Jed for a coffee and then go to Dryburgh Abbey on the River Tweed and look out over

Scott's view, named after Sir Walter Scott, who is reputed to have loved this view and is buried nearby. We would stop at Newcastle for lunch and finish at the Old Swan Hotel in Harrogate, where the doorman would be dressed in all his regalia with a hunting horn to welcome you to the hotel, like they did in the old days when you would arrive with a coach and horse.

Sunday saw me arriving home with my dirty washing, needing to sort myself out and to pack for tomorrow. I would hand in all my paperwork then pick up my passenger list and expenses for the twelve-day tour.

Ian followed me on the Dunoon tour and got the same treatment from Vi; however, instead of blowing it, he eventually married her. He did himself proud as she was a lovely girl. The next time I saw her I apologised (I think Ian put a good word in for me) and said it was only meant as a joke.

Whenever I was at the hotel from then on I would run all the staff up to a pub in the evening when they were off duty and we would have a good old time; they always looked forward to my arrival above any of the other touring companies, apart from when Ian was there to see Vi, of course. They became good friends to Janne and me over the years

Monday would see me back at Kings Cross to pick up a fresh crew of passengers to transport back to Harrogate, Baldock, Stamford and Doncaster. On Tuesday I would head back to Edinburgh via Scotch Corner, Newcastle and Jedburgh and then on Wednesday I would travel out to Perth and Blairgowrie, with its raspberry farms. I read in my *Blue Guide to Scotland* about the Beech hedge planted in 1746 which stands over eighty-five feet high and one mile long at Blairgowrie. I would always tell my passengers about it even though I didn't know where it was, until on one tour I thought 'blimey, that hedge is high' as I drove past, and then the penny dropped.

We would go to Glen Shee, up and round the Devil's Elbow, an 'S' bend two thousand feet above sea level, with a gradient of one in three, where people often stopped to watch the coaches negotiating it, then on to Braemar (where the highland games were hosted), stopping at Crathie Kirk church and looking at Balmoral Castle in the distance. Then we would head on to Ballater and the Huntley Arms Hotel in Aboyne.

On Thursday morning, before leaving we would have photographs taken and then drive back to the Bridge of Gairn and follow the road to Tomintoul, the highest village in the highlands, at 1,160 ft. We would encounter Spey Bridge, a monument to the commandos who were stationed there and the Cairngorms, the highest mountain range, with six peaks over 4,000 ft, ending at the Columba hotel at Inverness, capital of the Highlands.

Friday meant going down to Loch Ness, where we would look for the monster and I would do my talk about the loch being twenty-four miles long, 900 ft deep and never having been known to freeze. We would go past Urquhart Castle, said to be at the deepest part of the loch, the Kyle of Lochalsh, Glenelg and finally take the ferry over to Kyleakin on the Isle of Skye. We had to leave our coaches at Lochalsh as they were considered too big for the Skye roads. The ferrymen there always had a wee dram for the drivers (perhaps without the coaches they would not have had a job); but there is now a bridge.

On Saturday a local coach operator would come and take us on a tour of Skye, and as I had two days off I would go for the ride.

Sundays on Skye meant that everything stopped and so we were marooned as there was no way off the island. I remember one time a couple came to the hotel to say their guest house had refused to wait on them because it was a Sunday. Some drivers once hired a boat to take their passengers on a short boat trip on a Sunday and nearly caused a mutiny on the island.

I poached a list of stops for the tour from one of the senior drivers before I left London. It stated that on my way over to the Isle of Skye, about half-way between Invermoriston and the Kyle of Lochalsh, I would come to the Forres Hotel standing all alone; you could not miss it apparently, but I did.

From Invermoriston it was a single-track road until you got to the Kyle, with lay-bys for passing places. You had to motor along the track and if anything came your way the smaller vehicle would have to pull over to let the bigger one pass, and if I was holding cars up behind me I would pull over and let them pass.

After doing this for a while I saw in the distance a hotel, like an oasis, and said over the microphone that this must be our tea stop. But then I heard one elderly lady say to her friend beside me in the front seat that this was not the Forres Hotel she had stopped at before.

I thought, 'Well, I have not been on this road before, so maybe it's further on,' so I carried on past.

Then I heard her say, 'These are lovely views, I haven't been this way before.'

I pulled up and looked at them: 'What did you just say?'

'We haven't been this way before,' they replied, bewildered.

'Well how did you know that that wasn't the hotel you stayed in before?' I asked.

'Well, we stayed in the Forres Hotel in Forres.'

I apologised to the passengers and said, 'No tea stop today.' By the time I reached the Kyle they were a rushing for the toilets.

The following week the senior driver I spoke to stopped at the Forres Hotel and asked them if I had stopped. The manageress said, 'Stop? All we saw was a cloud of dust as he went past.' On my next twelve-day trip I had to explain what had happened.

On Monday we left Skye for Invergarry and went down Loch Lochy to Spean Bridge and Fort William, then on to Glen Coe and Oban. Tuesday was a free day.

Wednesday took us to Inveraray, around Loch Fyne and down Loch Lomond. We visited the picturesque villages of Luss and Balloch, leaving for our final stop at Windermere for the night.

We travelled to Buxton for the night on Thursday and on Friday we made our way through Bakewell, past the Rolls Royce factories at Derby, through Leicester, Luton, St Albans and then home.

This was repeated all through the summer. Some weeks had beautiful sunshine and so it was a pleasure to drive the people around, but others had heavy mist and fog so you could only tell the people what they were missing.

Once when I stopped for lunch at a hotel I turned the coach round so that we could have a quick exit when we were finished. I came out afterwards to see two elderly ladies trying to get into the coach through the emergency door at the back, which was really quite high; even I had a job to get in that way. One had her leg up in the air and her skirt raised and the other one had her shoulder under her posterior trying to lift her.

'What are you trying to do?' I asked.

'To get in the coach.'

'Well, why don't you use the proper door?'

'This was the side we got out of.'

'Yes, but I've turned the coach round and it's facing the other way now!'

'I told you, Maud,' one of them said. 'I knew it was easier to get in than this!'

What characters.

On one tour I had to stop in Glasgow, so I went to the local bus garage to find out where I could park for the night. The inspector said, 'You haven't left your coach unattended have you?'

'Why?' I asked.

'Get out there quick, otherwise they'll dismantle it,' he replied urgently.

I rushed out to find some little bare-footed urchins going through the coach and throwing all the personal luggage about; I had to chase them off. What a place!

The senior drivers had always told me, 'Never listen to the passengers,' but I got caught out once more. I was travelling through a big town (I can't remember where it is now) when one of the ladies sitting beside me pointed to her friend and said, 'There's the cathedral.' I glanced across to where she was indicating and saw this big church. 'I never knew there was a cathedral here,' I thought, and when I looked up the town in my *Blue Guide* it didn't mention a cathedral.

However, I had found from experience that you could tell the passengers anything and they would believe it, so from then on this town was a city and there was the cathedral. That is, until one tour when a lady came up to me and said, 'I used to live here and there is no cathedral.' So it became a town again.

On a similar note, I used to joke about Wigan pier when passing through, until again I had a lady tell me that Wigan does in fact have a pier. She said, 'If you give me your address I will send you a postcard with a picture of it,' and she did; it was of the canal.

We were sitting in the driver's rest room at the garage once, exchanging yarns about the passengers and their antics, when one of the drivers told a story about a lady and her daughter. Apparently he had stopped for morning coffee at a hotel where there was a lot of renovation work going on at the end of the coffee lounge. They were building new toilets downstairs, to save the passengers having to go upstairs all the time.

So the following week when they arrived at the hotel he explained that this was the coffee stop and anybody wanting the toilet should go to the end of the lounge. He said, 'It came to leaving time and those two could not be found, so I went to look for them. I then saw them coming out of the hotel and the lady was ranting and raving, saying, "I do not know what this country is coming to." She went on to explain that she had had one hell of a job getting onto the toilet and that her daughter had had to lift her on to it.

'I went to the manager for an explanation and he said, "The only explanation I can think of is that we haven't put the gents and ladies signs up yet, so she must have been in the gents trying to get on the urinal."'

It was getting near to the end of the season. My divorce was being finalised and I'd finished things with Anne. I was talking with the other drivers about this and one thing led to another until Ian asked, 'Have you got a girlfriend yet?'

I boasted: 'Yes, I've got them all over the country.'

'I've got a nice girl for you,' continued Ian. 'She's my girlfriend's friend, and also a divorcee. If it wasn't for my girlfriend, I would like to have gone out with her myself.'

The usual banter started with the drivers, and they said to Ian, 'Are you trying to get Al a date with one of those tarts you go out with?'

He took umbrage to the fact that he was trying to get me a date and they were mocking him. So he answered, 'Look, I wouldn't walk out with just anybody; if I say she's a nice girl then you can take it from me that she is.' Ian was a slim, good-looking, smart guy, and he did not take lightly to the drivers' comments.

The drivers started kidding me by saying, 'Well, Al, if she's that good what have you got to lose?'

When we were on tour I used to see Ian once every three weeks when we passed one another on the road. I always knew when I would be meeting him coming in the opposite direction to me, so I would tell my passengers to look out for the Christmas tree coming along. He would see me and then with headlights and spotlights blazing and hazard lights flashing we would pull up in the middle of the road, holding up all the traffic for a few minutes. He would extend his hand to shake mine, always coming out with some joke about have I got the socks I borrowed from him, and could he have them back. Another time he told me that the manager of the hotel which I had just left had phoned him, telling him to pass on the message that he didn't mind me taking the coat hangers, but could I leave the wardrobe there in future.

We were on the tankers during the winter so Ian and I saw a lot more of one another there, but he was not cut out for getting his hands dirty and eventually finished up as a rep for the oil trade.

Anyway, a date was arranged for me to pick up Ian and his girlfriend in Edmonton and then to go round to their friend Janne's, who was living with her mother.

She had just finished a summer season at Warner's holiday camp on the Isle of Wight, where she had worked as a receptionist in the day and on the bar in the evenings.

We proceeded to make our way to Southend, and on the way Ian said, 'Pull up at the Rayleigh Wier pub, I want to use the toilets.' So we all went to the loo, and then Ian said, 'We'll split the girls up and Janne can sit in the front with you.'

After spending the evening at Southend we made our way home. Janne had her hair in a bun and said to me, 'Do you mind if I let my hair down?'

'No,' I said, so she took out the clips and her hair fell round her shoulders – and I was gone.

I must say that I had a few, very nice girlfriends after Pat left me, but when I thought the time was right I packed them up; it was through no fault of their own, but because Pat had really hurt me and I wanted someone to pay, which was of course very unfair to the girls I met. But with Janne something clicked.

I didn't know what Janne thought of me, so a little time after this trip I tested the water by asking if she would like to come to Blackpool for the weekend and she answered 'Yes!' I forgot to say there would be fifty-three other people with us.

I was driving a party of my own family and friends down there that weekend. The only problem was that all the seats were taken up, so we took a dining-room table chair and put it beside myself and the others at the front and

Janne sat there for most of the journey, although now and again someone would give her a rest and swap seats. The weekend went well and my family and friends all said what a nice girl Janne was.

By the time we came home from this the coach season was just about finished, so I prepared myself for the tankers again, only now it was different.

Janne lived in Edmonton, north of London and I was in Stratford. The work on the tankers had increased so much that I was up at five o'clock in the morning to go to Barking to start work at six. I would then chase about like a lunatic all day and not finish until seven or eight at night and then come home, only for the whole thing to start again the next day; so I was not seeing much of Janne.

However, soon she managed to get a bed sit in Forest Gate to be nearer to me and she found a job locally. Some time later we got a one-bedroom downstairs flat near to my parents and Janne lived there while I stayed at home for a bit longer.

We started doing up the flat and one Saturday evening, when we had been decorating until late, by the time I left to go home it was about midnight. I said goodnight to Janne, ran down the side of the house and jumped over the front garden wall to leg it home. However, as I jumped over the wall, I noticed a car coming up behind me, which turned out to be a police car. It drove along the side of me and the policeman told me to stop.

Two policemen got out: 'Where are you running to?'

'Home,' I replied, pointing to the house over the road.

'We have reason to think that you came out of that house there.'

'Yes, it's my fiancée's house.'

'Well, we will take you back to prove it.'

So we walked back. I got the key out of my pocket and opened the door, shouting to Janne that it was only me with two police officers. She came out to see what the trouble was.

One of the officers said, 'You didn't tell us that you had a key.'

'You didn't ask me. You asked if I could prove I came out of the house.'

'We're sorry to have disturbed you, Miss,' he said to Janne, and continued to me: 'We want your name and address.'

'What for?'

'Well, tomorrow you might want to complain about us stopping you.'

I started back at Aero soon after and met up with all of the familiar faces who wanted to know about my summer season, and I do believe some of the drivers were a little jealous. I carried on with the black oil deliveries in the old and faithful Atkinson eight-legger which had stood idle for six months.

One of my first deliveries was to Wandsworth swimming baths. It had recently been renovated and the whole thing was spotlessly clean, even the boiler house (I think this was because the boilermen were usually ex-seamen stokers, and cleanliness seemed to be their thing). All the Dignity from the town council had arrived to see the new oil burners fired up. They seemed quite proud of their achievements in restoring the baths.

They told me to connect up and wait for the signal before I started pumping, and eventually the boilerman came out and said, 'OK driver, you can start now.' So I jumped into the cab, started the engine and engaged the pto (power take off). I had been pumping for a short time, when I realised there was panic on everyone's faces and cries of, 'Shut it off! Shut it off!' I jumped back in the cab, disengaged the pto and got out to see what the problem was.

They informed me that there was a leak under the fuel tank and that all the oil was running out of the bottom. I walked into the boiler house and saw that there was oil all over the previously spotlessly clean floor. It looked like a total disaster, especially because you cannot clean it up easily, as it becomes like tar when it goes cold, so you have to use sand and a shovel.

I had to tell all the celebrities that I had another shock for them, because as all my hoses were full and I had to clear them, more oil was going to come in. They asked if there was any way I could do it without getting more oil everywhere and I said, 'Yes, if you want a mess in the street as well,' which I knew they would decline. I thought, 'In for a penny, in for a pound,' and blew my hoses clear. When I left, it looked a total mess; I didn't go back again after it was all sorted.

We had a new driver come to us from the coaches who had many such incidents. He was taken out training with one of the regular drivers and after a while was let loose on his own. For some unknown reason he just kept forgetting to open the delivery valve and so kept blowing his hoses; in the end he had a permanent clear-up crew following him around. To overcome this problem they gave him a mate and at their first delivery the driver said, 'Make sure that valve is opened before we start pumping.' They both got quite excited after having made the delivery and walked into the office to get their delivery note signed. They were getting in the tanker to start driving away, when there was an almighty crash. When they got out to see what had happened, they realised they had forgotten to uncouple the delivery hoses.

They had managed to pull the tank pipe work away from the customer's tank and the oil that had been in the pipe was running all over the ground; but the driver was not worried as his clear-up crew were following up behind them.

The next day they went out and forgot that they had stretched the hose the day before, so as soon as they started pumping the hose blew again; the clear-up crew was therefore given a permanent job. 'Another nail in the coffin for the coach drivers,' I thought.

On another occasion this driver opened the valve before connecting his hose, so that more oil was all over the ground. He became a standing joke with the drivers and if you were unfortunate enough to be given a delivery after he had been there, you found yourself tramping about in thick tar which was all around the filler pipe.

Work was picking up all the time and more new vehicles were coming to the garage. Another two eight-wheel AEC Mammoth Majors Mk Vs (4,000 gallon) came home for bridging from Thames Haven to the depot at Barking and were expected to do three loads a day. They were bringing in 12,000 gallons each, which meant a maximum of 24,000 gallons. But that was not enough, so two trailers were ordered which could carry 1,500 gallons, to be pulled by the eight-wheelers. However, the drivers' speed was reduced to twenty miles per hour when towing a trailer so they could only do two loads a day. This brought in 11,000 a day, making the total 22,000 gallons, dropping 2,000 gallons short; so that idea went out the window and so did the trailers.

It was around this time that I began suffering with constant catarrh. My GP was drowning me in nasal drops, but they were just not working. I made another appointment to see him, although when I got there I found that it was a locum doctor, and he diagnosed polyps. I told him that my seasonal job would be starting in April and he said, 'I'll get you into hospital as soon as possible.'

I was admitted to Whipps Cross hospital, where I met some old-boy patients who told me I had nothing to worry about, I would be in the theatre for about an hour and then when I came round I would look like I had run into the back of a bus, with two black eyes and a sticking plaster over my nose. 'Thank you very much', I said. I then happened to notice a man in the corner bed who had a diseased cheek bone; he had a scar from the corner of his eye to his mouth and it was not a pretty sight.

The doctor came to give me a pre-medical check and asked if I had any questions, so I said, 'Yes, let's get one thing right, Doc. I don't want to finish up like the man in the corner bed, otherwise you can forget it.'

'What man?' he asked and I pointed him out.

He started laughing: 'He has something totally different to you.'

'Yes, but once I am under the anaesthetic you might decide to carry on.'

The doctor must have thought I was a proper nutter, but I was just warning him.

When I came round after the operation, I had nuns sitting at the side of the bed, holding my hands and looking very worried as they could not stop the bleeding. I thought, 'Bloody hell, he went along with it anyway, even after I warned him.' The nuns got in touch with the surgeon and asked him why my nose had not been packed, and he told them that it was such a clean operation they had decided not to do it, but to keep putting ice packs round my face to get the blood to congeal. I was put down as a bleeder.

So I came out and was ready for my summer season on the coaches again.

Alex with his Dad – and his International truck - outside their house in Stratford, east London, in about 1937.

Alex and his friends took a Morris 8 saloon to Devon in the early 1950s.

In 1953 Alex joined the RAF for his national service. He quickly became a Driver.
In the top picture he is seated at the front, on the right.
He is on the left in the bottom picture.

Alex spent several years driving buses for London Transport, just as RTs (left, on the skid pan) were giving way to Routemasters (below). He had previously had a spell on trolleybuses, a time that yielded some memorable stories.
(Photos courtesy Syd Eade).

GALLEON COACH TOURS

Tour No. 178 — South Devon and Cornwall

Alex carried out many coach tours for Galleon, covering the West Country, Wales and Scotland.

Alex's fund of information included the correct pronunciation (from memory) of the full name of Llanfair PG. The ticket is from 1964.

Letters of appreciation made the job especially fulfilling...

BRITISH RAILWAYS BOARD (M)

BR 4405

LLANFAIRPWLLGWYNGYLLGOGERYCHWYRNDROBWLLLLANTYSILIOGOGOGOCH

B 17418

PLATFORM TICKET 3d.

AVAILABLE ONE HOUR ON DAY OF ISSUE ONLY
NOT VALID IN TRAINS. NOT TRANSFERABLE.

FOR CONDITIONS SEE OVER

| 1 | 2 | 3 | 4 | 5 | 6 | 7 | 8 | 9 | 10 | 11 | 12 |

17418

B

It was a lovely trip, but the best tour can be a failure without a steady, cheerful, efficient courier – thank you, Alec, and will you accept the enclosed material

Arriving in Scotland and soon to face the narrow, twisting roads right on the edge of Loch Lomond.

One of the many light-hearted moments on the tours.

Alex and Janne, in the centre of the picture at the back, enjoyed a mock marriage at Gretna Green.

After a few seasons on the coaches, Alex found regular work with Bowen Petroleum.

In 1967 Alex moved on to work for Gulf, a job he was to hold for nearly thirty years.

Alec with his Gulf tanker.

In retirement, Alex has kept his hand in as a driver. He and another volunteer painted and drove these ex-BOAC Leyland Atlanteans.

Janne and Alex.

Chapter 9

Round Four

IAN and I started back on the Scotch tours, and Vi went back to the hotel for the summer season.

I started on my first twelve-day of the season to the Isle of Skye. After leaving Inverness I was running along Loch Ness, telling the passengers about the size, width, depth and any other information I had about the loch and, of course, Nessy. As we approached Urquhart Castle, where Nessy is supposed to be sometimes seen, looking down at the loch, we suddenly saw something sticking out of the water and moving along leaving a wash. I joked to the passengers that they were in luck today, but then I noticed that all the traffic was stopping for a better view.

I pulled over to the side of the road and we all jumped out, but by then it had disappeared. There was a green-grocer's lorry nearby with its driver standing on the cab roof, so I said to him, 'Is that Nessy?'

'I don't know, but I travel this road four times a day and I've never seen anything like that before.'

On our evening meal stop at Fort Augustus Hotel I went to the Abbey and told the Abbot what I had seen. 'Most definitely, that was Nessy,' he replied. 'I've written books on Nessy and I'll give you some copies.' I still have those books.

He always appreciated my taking my passengers in

because they bought souvenirs and in return for this he gave me two beautiful St Christophers, the patron saint of travel. However, while I was away one time my father took my car in for a service and they were taken, never to be seen again.

We made our money on the road by putting the passengers on boat rides on the lochs or by taking them to places such as the woollen mills and the distilleries. It may have been that we sometimes cut things out so as to get them where we knew we could earn a couple of shillings extra.

On one such tour a passenger made himself known to me and told me that he owned a haulage firm in the East End of London. He said that if ever I decided to give up the coaches there was always a job with him. 'Thank you very much,' I replied.

After dinner at Inverness I took my passengers to the highland dancing. I got chatting about Nessy to an elderly lady who lived on the lochside and she told me that she would never go in a boat on the loch. She said there was even a young girl who had tried to swim the loch but had to be taken out because she said that there was something sinister about it.

I left the Grosvenor Hotel, Edinburgh on a bright and sunny morning and headed south for our overnight stop at the Old Swan Hotel in Harrogate. When I arrived at the Old Swan I was met by one of the senior drivers from Galleon who said, 'Come and have a drink, you've earned it.'

'I would rather go to my room and get showered,' I replied, 'and then come down and have a drink. I'm soaked in sweat.' (There was not a lot of ventilation in the front of the coaches and we had a glass panel in the roof.)

But he insisted, so we went to the bar. 'What do you want to drink?' he asked.

'A pint of lager.'

The other driver had the same. When the barman had given us our drinks my friend said, 'Now, pay the man and I'll see you in the dining room for dinner.' With that, he walked off.

So after I showered I returned downstairs where we sat at a table in the dining room. The wine waiter came to the table. 'Any drinks?' he asked.

My friend asked me what I wanted, so I replied: 'A pint of lager.'

He then asked the waiter how much a pint of lager was and when the waiter told him he said, 'Get him half.' What workmates I had!

We were even warned by the garage manager not to lend money to other drivers as we might not get it back from them. Before each tour we were given petty cash for diesel and other things we might need on the tour, such as tips for the hotel porters. However, some drivers would use it for betting, or drink the money away, and would then come and ask you to lend them some because they needed diesel to get home.

I got caught out myself by a driver one year. He was not one of the regular drivers, he was one of those who would appear at the start of the year and then leave half-way through the season. We were in the hotel bar and he said he did not have enough money for diesel and could I lend him £50. I thought, 'Well, he is a driver like me and you should help one another on the road.' In any case, I had no cause to doubt him.

He said he would leave the money at the garage as he was home a day before me. When I got home and told the manager he said, 'He's packed the job in and gone.'

'What about my money?'

'You've lost that,' he said. 'What did I tell you about lending money to other drivers? They are given the same as you, so there's no need for anyone to borrow.' So from then on I was the hard man. I liked to use my money more wisely. Every evening I would phone Janne and see if she would like anything nice while I was away and I would always buy it for her.

At the end of the seasons we would make it known at the woollen mills and other stops that we were finished for the season and they would pay us out, or give us things to the same value. (When we took parties into the shops they would note down how much was spent and then give us a percentage.)

Just before the season came to an end I had a party of Australian sheep farmers on the tour. I asked one of them what he thought of the sheep we have in this country.

He looked at me and said, 'Sheep! You don't call them black-faced little wretches sheep. Back in Australia we call them underground mutton. Do you know what that is?'

'No.'

'Rabbit,' he finished.

Janne and I made arrangements to have a quiet wedding at the register office in Edmonton with her brothers and sister as witnesses; we had both been through the razzmatazz of a big wedding and nothing had come of either of them. My mother and father were a bit upset but wished us well, and as we would be living in the flat we had found in the road opposite them, they were not getting rid of us.

At the end of this break between seasons I began preparing myself for the return to Aero Petroleum, though I was not sure about staying there much longer. The workload was increasing every year and there was also the weather to contend with: the colder the weather, the more work there was. I really didn't enjoy it and the hours were so long. Over the course of the winter months I had been soaked to the skin, brought to a standstill in snow drifts and frozen from the cold. It was a total contrast to the summer season: one minute I was practically on holiday and the next I was out in all weathers.

I was out one night delivering in Kent and it got to about seven in the evening when I really had had enough. I phoned the office and told him I still had two deliveries to do and he said, 'Well, stay the night and do them in the morning.'

'No, I don't want a night out here, I'm coming home.'

But he said, 'Come on, you must be just like the rest. They want the night-out money but they don't want to actually spend the night out.'

This was true of a lot of the workers. I was on the tankers for thirty-five years in total and never knew any driver to have a night out. On paper some may have, but I was always in my own bed. The problem was it was harder for the seasonal drivers like me, as finding the addresses and delivery points took a lot longer than for the regular drivers who knew all the deliveries by heart.

I got back to the depot, parked the tanker up and placed my tickets in the office with a note saying where the product was and what compartment. I then got in my car and came home. I was shattered; I think that if I'd I carried on I would have had a nervous breakdown. I had become so disillusioned with the job; I never stopped all day and would have nothing to eat or drink just to make sure I could get the work done.

I phoned the office the next day and said I wouldn't be returning.

I decided to give the buses another go, so I applied and was quickly accepted. I started training at West Ham again, only this time they had AEC RT and RTL Leyland buses. They were also waiting for the new Routemaster buses, or what were known as the RMs.

After finishing the training and passing the tests I was back on the road. I really enjoyed driving the buses as there was no worry attached to the job and at the end of my shift I could go home, which I was never far from, instead of being stuck out in the wilderness somewhere. I felt much more relaxed.

I was put on the route twenty-five: Becontree to Victoria. I had been on the buses for about a week when I had to take a bus over at good old Findon Road (how could I ever forget it). I was introducing myself to the conductor when I happened to notice a gold badge inspector also waiting for a bus at the same stop, but I quickly forgot about him as my bus came up and I had to speak to the driver who informed me that all was well.

I got in, adjusted the seat and started the bus, and when my conductor was settled he gave me the bell and we were away. We were going to Bow Road bus garage, back to Becontree and then Victoria. As I pulled into Bow bus garage I jumped down and went round the back to speak to the conductor. As I got there I was shocked to see the gold badge inspector sitting there. He said, 'Mr Heymer, I have come to see how you are getting on and to assess your driving.' He continued, 'You gave a smooth ride with no excessive jolting, but I have one complaint, and that is that not once did you use the handbrake. Now, if your foot slipped off the brake you would have an accident; but apart from that, good luck for the future!' I said thank you and off he went.

When my father taught me to drive he had told me to sit in the corner of the seat, so when I started driving professionally I got in no end of rows with the instructors who wanted me to sit straight. However, when I did I felt lost and couldn't drive, so they eventually relented and I sat side-saddle. They haughtily informed me that they did not want cowboys driving their buses, but the conductors always said they could tell what sort of a drive they would get as soon as a driver got in the cab and sat down, and they should know.

When I was on Routemasters I found that the best way to drive them was manually as, although it was an automatic gearbox, no two buses were the same. Some would be in top gear at twenty-three miles per hour and struggling. I used to put it in first gear and then drive flat out in each gear through the box to get the maximum speed.

The gear lever was on the left side of the steering column and the neutral was vertical from roof to floor, so I would push the gear lever down towards the floor and forward to engage first gear, drive flat out in that gear, and with the finger tips of my left hand flick the gear lever back towards me for second gear. When I flicked it forward again it would enter neutral and jump up the gate where I flicked it forward for third gear and then back to me for fourth. I wanted the bus to change gear when I wanted it to, otherwise it would be up and down the gearbox like a yo-yo.

Later, when I had my own conductress, she told me that her friend had been on my bus and passed a remark about how fast I got the bus moving.

However, it was not always so smooth. Back when I still had a male conductor, I once started off from the bus stop and went through my usual drill. I was flat out in second gear and about to change into third, when I flicked the gear lever and the bus nearly stood on its nose. I nearly catapulted myself out through the windscreen and all the old dears fell over with their shopping and started shouting, 'What are you doing? Did you get out of bed the wrong way this morning? Has your wife upset you?'

I sat there trying to figure out what had happened. It was as if I had applied the brakes, but I had not touched them; then I realised what had happened: the gear lever had gone straight back into first gear. The conductor told me later that he had explained to the passengers that these new buses always played up in the rain, and it was not until some time later that they said, 'What are you talking about? It's not raining.'

One feature of the Routemaster was that they had sliding driver doors as opposed to outward opening, to ensure safer entry and exit of the bus. So in hot weather you could drive with the door open.

I was a spare driver for quite a while so I would have a different conductor each day. One of these conductors said to me once, 'Instead of going to Ilford, let's have ourselves some extra time in the canteen and go straight to Victoria.'

'What about the people waiting at Ilford for the bus.'

'Oh, they can catch the next one,' he said.

Another conductor, when we were running into the depot from Victoria, said, 'When we get to Stratford, instead of going through Green Street and along the Barking road to the depot, we will cut through West Ham Lane and into the depot that way.' Unfortunately for me it was the West Ham dog racing night and the buses were queuing up at Plaistow Station for railway passengers to take them to the stadium. As I was about to pass the stationary buses an inspector jumped out in front of me and pulled me in, wanting an explanation as to why I was off route.

The only way I could defend myself was to say that I was new, so he said, 'Well, in future read the timetable properly. I will be watching out for you.' The conductor never said a word and didn't come to my defence so from then on I took no notice of what he said. The conductors were always ducking and diving and pulling stunts so that they could finish early or save working too hard.

Some bus drivers and conductors thought it was their given right to hail and stop buses in between stops or to always stand on the platform talking to the conductor. I never thought about practising this; I would have been too embarrassed if the bus hadn't stopped.

When I did allow it to happen I was really angry afterwards. It was on one late evening, in the dark and rain. I had left Barking Station heading for Becontree and as I was passing some shops a figure appeared from a shop doorway and hailed me to stop. I recognised a man in a bus uniform, so I eased up for him to get on, but he made me stop completely. Then out from the shop came his wife and four children to get on, the bus stop being some way away. To say the least I was quite annoyed that he thought he could stop a bus to pick up his family where and when he pleased. My conductor, Iris, was annoyed too and said as much when we got to Becontree terminus.

Oxford Street always caused problems for me. When driving through it I used to slow down and try to read the bus numbers to see which stop was mine, but in the end I just stopped anywhere, as there were so many I never knew which mine was. I used to leave Victoria and not stop until I got to Oxford Street; my conductor loved it and one day said, 'Do you know you missed about six stops?'

'No,' I said. It was because you were left to find your stops yourself; they didn't show you that when you were training. You should have seen the rush when I went to the wrong stop.

I then got my own conductress, whom I mentioned earlier. She was a nice girl called Iris and I tried to look after her as all the drivers did with their conductors; you were a crew and a working party after all. So, if we were dominoed out in the rush hour, I would take it slowly so that she could get her fares in. Also, as you would do the same shift all week you got to know which drivers were in front and which were behind, so to make things easier I would see myself away from stops and rush into others, so that the bus behind would pass by and stop at the next stop. We would leap frog with one another to clear the stops. But of course, the stop you went past would always be the one where somebody wanted to get off, so you would stop short to let them off and go round the other bus at the stop.

I would see Janne as soon as I finished work, and when I had a rest day we would have the whole day together, even though she also had a job.

I had reached thirty now, and Janne twenty-three; the coaches were beckoning and I had itchy feet. Janne begged me not to go back, but I explained to her all the money which I could make on tour. She was not convinced, so I got Ian and Vi to meet us for a drink and persuade her to let me because of the money we could save. On tour it didn't cost me a thing to live as everything was paid for by the company, plus I made extra money on the road. She always relented in the end, but I used to hate coming home for one night because in the morning she would cry and say, 'Don't go back.' But I had to; people were expecting to be taken on their holidays.

I handed my notice in at the buses and they were upset as I now had all types of PSV licence. When I was called into the office by the depot manager, he said that now I had the licence I was going to leave, just as so many other drivers did. Yet I informed him that if he looked at my details he would note I had the licence before I came on the buses, although granted I only had single-deckers then.

Despite my comings and goings, a lot of the drivers whom I had met when I was on the trolleybuses said, 'We haven't seen you for a while; we must have been on different shifts.' When I told them that I had in fact left and come back they seemed very surprised.

Chapter 10

Round Five

SO I happily started back ready for another season with the coaches, along with all the other seasonal and regular drivers, including my friend Ian. We were still great friends; at the end of the previous season Janne and I had gone away with Ian and Vi to Cornwall for a two-week holiday.

As I have mentioned before, Ian was a one-off; once seen never forgotten. He was slim with dark black hair and extremely good looking; he had the personality to go with it too. I had been going to my local for years and had never got to know the guv'nor's name, but that changed one Christmas when Ian and Vi came to see us and he took me to the local for a drink.

We had straight Scotch (we had got used to it from the Scottish tours where we were always offered the wee dram) and drink for drink I matched him. Before long Ian was playing the piano and singing on the microphone, and the next thing I knew he was kissing the Mrs of the pub under the mistletoe. Luckily, even the guv'nor was laughing. Ian pointed at me and said to him, 'Look at him, he's as pissed as me, but he won't let himself go.' I nodded and promised him I would walk out straight as a die, which I did.

'He won't embarrass himself,' Ian said.

All the hotels loved Ian as he really was the spice of life. I used to keep in contact with him by phone during the tours until we inevitably met on the road, all the lights blazing as usual. We would always stop and hold the traffic up while he shook my hand and passed some quip to make the passengers laugh. I got into a routine of telling jokes and having a laugh with them.

Sometimes when it was quiet, to make conversation I would pull the mike down and say, 'Has anybody noticed those small trees on the top of the hills that stand alone?' and there was always someone who would say yes.

I would say, 'Well, they are known as Charlie trees. During the battles with the English, Bonny Prince Charlie had to find means of escape, so he got all the landowners who were for his cause to plant a tree on their topmost hill and then he knew where he could take refuge. That's why they are called Charlie trees.'

I overheard a passenger say, 'I think he takes us for a load of Charlies.' I had to hide my laughter.

After our afternoon lunch stops I would stop the joking and get the coach to go at a steady pace so that the drone of the engine would send them to sleep.

One Friday night, while in the hotel at Edinburgh on my last nine-day tour, I received a phone call from the manager to say he wanted me home a day early to do a Devon and Cornwall tour leaving on the Sunday, so after dropping my people off at Harrogate I would continue home. My passengers were not too happy about losing me, but I left at about 5.30 and headed straight home, getting in about midnight. The next morning I was on my way to Torquay.

I felt bad for Janne as we only met for two evenings every three weeks. By the time I had got back to the garage, handed in my papers and collected my next tour papers, it was often eight o'clock before I got away. Janne and I would go for a drink and then the next morning I would be off again. I was so torn between going and staying at home all the time that I was starting to think about looking elsewhere.

On top of this, I used to do over a thousand miles a week. As this was before most motorways were opened, I was driving over some very dodgy single tracks and hilly roads. I would always come home with not a scratch on the coach, but then damage would be done in the garage overnight, anyway.

At the end of the coach season some of the drivers went on Bowen's, an independent oil company and the main blue paraffin distributor in north London for the Esso petroleum company. I applied for work there but was told that I was too late as they had their number of drivers needed, so I had to look elsewhere. I then thought about applying to be a driving test examiner and sent off for the appropriate forms, which duly arrived, but after reading them and seeing what they wanted to know, I decided to give it a miss.

Round the corner from where we lived was a small haulage company, so I walked round to see if they wanted drivers.

The guv'nor said that yes, they did want a driver, but that they could not take me on until a new lorry had arrived at the garage. So I said, 'Well, I'm not doing anything, so I will be available when you want me.'

Then, one morning at about six there was a bang on the door and I opened it to find the guv'nor of this place standing there. He said, 'Do you still want a job?'

'Yes.'

'Well, get dressed and come round as soon as you can.'

My father was not happy about me working for this firm because one of their lorries had knocked over and killed my eight-year-old cousin in the Bow Road. It was probably not the driver's fault, as my cousin had run across the traffic lights when they were in the driver's favour, but the family was devastated, and my father said, 'Don't ever mention to my family you're driving for that firm.' I told him it was for only a short time, until the coaches started again.

I was taken for a driving test by the fitter in a seven-ton S-type Bedford with helper springs which brought it up to a ten-tonner. On returning, he told the guv'nor I was all right, so he gave me a piece of paper (not a proper pick-up note) with an address in Barking and said, 'Go there and they will tell you where to go.'

When I arrived at this address, a man said, 'Take this parcel to this address in Slough.' So I threw it in the cab, delivered it and returned to the yard.

This happened for the next three days: picking up an item from somewhere and delivering it somewhere else, and they would always fit in the cab. So, on my arrival back at the yard I asked the guv'nor if I could use his car instead of taking the lorry. He asked why, and I said, 'Well, so far I have not used the back end of the lorry, only the cab.'

'I was giving you time to settle in because you have just come off the buses,' he said.

'No, I haven't just come off the buses.'

'Oh, well, in that case, pick up this ten ton of steel in the morning.' Ouch.

So I picked up steel, timber and all sorts; sometimes it even had to go on the bolster over the cab and I would think, 'I hope it doesn't come through the cab.'

My most memorable load was when I had to go to a scrap metal yard where they told me to go on the weighbridge.

When I came off the weighbridge they put some brass ingots on, then I had to go back on the weighbridge and then off again as they put another metal load on, and so on, each time having the metal weighed. I was getting giddy going on and off the bridge, but it was not until I was loaded that they really frightened me.

They said, 'Whatever you do, don't stop anywhere, and keep looking in the mirrors to see if you think you're being followed.'

I was shitting myself, but I delivered it to the smelting foundry and wasn't sorry to be unloaded.

I had another memorable encounter with this company when I had to go to a slaughterhouse and they just threw all the waste meat, bones and carcasses onto the lorry for me to take to Rotherhithe railway arches, where a bulk tipper would pick it up and take it to a glue factory. On the way there everybody was holding their noses and looking at me in disgust. As soon as I got back to the yard I got the water hose and washed out the back, but it stank for ages.

I used to see my father most evenings and he would say, 'Where have you been today, son?' and I would tell him. Then I would ask him where he had been and he would answer, 'You haven't seen the skies where I have been today, son.'

I would say, 'You silly old sod, they had to get you a lorry nearer the ground because you cannot climb up in the cab now,' (he had a low loader) and we would both laugh.

After a few months of this I had to get Ian and Vi to invite us out for a drink to once again talk Janne into letting me return to the coaches for another season.

Chapter 11

Round Six

JANNE agreed once more, so I returned again and was promoted to a seven-day all round Wales tour and allocated an AEC Reliance with a Plaxton body. I did a couple of Devon and Cornwall spring tours and then began my Welsh tour. Through the summer, whenever I could, I took Janne with me to Scotland or Wales so that she could get a holiday and to show her how well I lived when I was away.

I missed seeing Ian on the road as he was doing the seven-day Lakes tour, but we kept in touch over the phone, and now that we both came home on Sunday the four of us could meet up for a chat and a drink, until we were away again on Monday.

I was once loading at Kings Cross and had my head in the boot of the coach sorting out the cases when I felt a tap on my shoulder. I looked around to see the man who had been sitting in the front of the coach with me when I had the accident in Scotland. In my heart I had known this might happen one day. We exchanged niceties and he said he was coming with me to Wales.

I said, 'I expect you'll change your mind now,' but he was very forgiving and said it was just one of those things.

'My wife and I are looking forward to travelling with you again,' he added. I felt my nightmare was over.

On Mondays my overnight stop was Barry Island in South Wales. So I made my way out of Kings Cross to Beaconsfield for coffee, stopping briefly at Gloucester for lunch and down the A48 to Lydney, which had a very steep hill. Later, when I was on the tankers, a tanker driver was killed on it when his brakes faded. I would carry on to Chepstow for tea and finally to Barry.

Our Tuesday night stop was Milford Havon. On the way there we would go out through Llantwit Major, Bridgend, Port Talbot (where the steel works were), Swansea, Llanelli for coffee, and then to Carmarthen across the River Towy (where you could see the coracle fishing boats) for lunch and Tenby for tea.

In the morning, before leaving for Aberystwyth, I arranged for the passengers to have their photographs taken as a party, for prints to be delivered to us at our hotel in Llandudno. We then left by Haverfordwest, where we made our way to St Davids, which had one of the largest and finest cathedrals in Wales. This road was famous for its seventeen hills over sixteen miles. On our coffee stop we would often encounter rooks sitting on the cathedral wall looking for something to steal.

We went through Fishguard, Cardigan and many more places, before reaching Aberystwyth. On Thursday we went to Machynlleth and Dolgellau along Lake Bala. On my first trip out there I was looking for suitable coffee stops and stopped in the little town of Bala, by the lake. I noticed a nice coffee house and enquired if they could accommodate fifty people every week during the summer. She was a very charming lady and said we were more than welcome. I asked where I could park the coach and was directed to the town car park.

I drove in to the car park, which was empty apart from

one lorry in the middle, so I thought I would park next to it. I pulled past him and started to reverse alongside, when all of a sudden the coach stopped abruptly and I wondered why. I looked in both of the outside mirrors and could see nothing, and then I peered into the interior mirror and could not believe what I had done.

I had backed into a telegraph pole. The car park was like a desolate airfield and I had managed to back into a pole. I looked through the windscreen and could see the tele-phone wires jumping up and down. 'Who would put a telegraph pole in the middle of a car park?' I thought; only the Welsh.

When I arrived home I told the garage that I had backed into a small post and creased the rear bumper. They said, 'Don't worry; we'll get you a new one for next week.'

After I had made my mark at Bala I crossed the country to Trawsfynydd, with its huge reservoir and dam, and then up to Blaenau Ffestiniog, with all the slate quarries. At Betws-y-Coed we would have a short stop at the water-falls, before going through the Llanberis pass, to Snowdon for tea and finally to Llandudno.

Friday was a free day, so in the evening I arranged a trip to the local theatre, where we could get a percentage off the tickets.

On Saturday we would go through places such as St Asaph, down the Horseshoe Pass, to Llangollen for coffee, to the Forest of Dean for afternoon tea and for a boat ride on the River Wye. When I spoke to the boatman he told me that the boat would only turn right; what a laugh, I daren't tell the passengers.

When we were in Llangollen for our tea stop, there happened to be three others from my company there too. I was the first one away and came out to find my coach empty. The company was changing its colours and I had one of the coaches in the new colours, so all my passengers were sitting on one of the other coaches. I got on to join them and said, 'Everybody enjoy their break?' and they said yes. So I said, 'How long have we been together now?

'Four days.'

'And you still don't know the colour of my coach!' They started laughing when I pointed to my coach and said, 'That's ours.'

All the time you had to watch out for passengers getting on the wrong coach. It used to happen especially when we loaded at Kings Cross; they would give you their cases and then get on the coach next to you.

Essex County Coaches was contracted to operate tours for the Workers Travel Association. On the side of these coaches was a Galleon ship with 'W.T.A.' in the sails, but this did not go down well with the passengers, as when you were in the hotels waiting to go in for dinner the head waiter would call out names such as Wallace Arnold, Glentons, and then the Workers Travel Association. This did not sound very good in comparison, so in time they changed to Galleon tours.

After Llangollen we would carry on to the Chase Hotel at Ross-on-Wye for an overnight stop. In this hotel they had a room with Noele Gordon's name on the door (the well-known actress from *Coronation Street*), as apparently she often stayed there. On Sunday we would head back home, ready to do it all again on Monday, and this would carry on until the end of September.

There was a sense of community out on the roads. I was once travelling along on the way home and just happened to notice a Buxted meat lorry pass me. I didn't think much about it, but then the following week I passed him again, at roughly the same spot. I still didn't think much about it, but then I started to notice it every week and he must have noticed me. After a few of these meetings he gave me a little wave and from then on it was a cheery wave and flashing lights as we came in sight of each other. We never met, but I suppose we felt ourselves to be knights of the road.

I had a less cheerful encounter once when I was on a country lane and came upon a farmer herding his cows towards me. I had to stop, but as I did so the cows surrounded the coach. They walked slowly by, but one bright spark came right to the front of the coach and stared up at me, then, as it started to walk away, it swung its behind up against the coach so that the headlight fell out and smashed to the ground. I hastily jumped out and approached the farmer who looked at me with a glazed expression, putting his hands up as though to say there was nothing he could do. When I got back to the depot they said, 'A likely story.'

On another occasion on the country roads I had a very strange experience. There was a railway strike and I was late leaving Kings Cross so I wanted somewhere I could push the coach to the limit to make up time. I came to this nice wide, straight road, with no other traffic about, so I gave it the gun. I was really motoring along when from nowhere a dog came out of a field. There was nothing I could do; the front nearside of the coach hit the dog and it went spinning through the air like a bullet out of a gun.

I stopped as soon as I could and a couple of men from the coach and I went back looking in the hedgerows for it, but there was no animal to be seen, apart from this one dog sitting down by the side of a tractor being stroked by the farmer. I approached the farmer and asked if it was his dog and if it was all right. 'Well, he seems to be,' he said. I explained that I had just hit a dog with the coach and the farmer replied, 'Well, he is the only dog around here, so it must have been him.' More time had been lost.

A funnier moment happened in September, towards the end of the summer tours, when it was getting rather chilly. We were going along the road quite merrily until the silence was broken with shouts of 'Fire! Fire! The coach is on fire!' I pulled up, evacuated the coach and got back in to see where the fire was. I could not find anything, so I asked the man who was doing all the shouting to tell me where he thought the fire was, and he said, 'It's coming from under the seat.'

I replied, 'Don't worry. It was a bit chilly so I put the heaters on and one of them is right under you.' He was full of apologies and a little embarrassed. All the passengers were laughing.

Around the time that the autumn tours were starting I stood outside the office talking to the fitter about where he was going for his holiday, which happened to be Butlins. There were only him and his wife he said, and they went every year. 'I've never been to a holiday camp,' I replied. Just then the manager came out the office: 'You are away on Monday, on a tour of the holiday camps,' he said. He must have been ear-wigging.

So on Monday I loaded up and headed for Paignton and Pontin's holiday camps where we were staying for three nights, doing little tours during the day. We were staying at Paignton first, in wooden shacks, and on the first morning over the tannoy came, 'Last one for breakfast in the morning gets chucked in the pool!' I thought, 'I cannot swim,' so I was first in the queue every morning; they wouldn't catch me.

After three days we moved on to Chichester and had three nights in Pontin's.

The accommodation was much better there as we were in brick-built chalets. I was glad the tour did it this way round, as if we had left these chalets to go to those wooden shacks I think there might have been a mutiny.

One day I had to take them to Portsmouth ferry for a tour around the Isle of Wight. I pulled up outside the station, which meant parking on a small pier, and announced to the ticket collector that Galleon tours was here. He said, 'Where are your passengers?'

'Sitting on the coach.'

He looked out of the window and shouted, 'Get that coach off the pier! It's a three ton weight limit, and if the police catch you, they'll nick you.' So I made a hasty retreat and the passengers had to walk back to the station.

I went off and parked the coach quickly, but when I got back the ferry was just leaving and my passengers were shouting to me, 'Jump!' I thought, 'You must be joking. I'll catch the next ferry.'

When I got there I found that my people had gone on a local coach hire for the trip. I thought, 'Bloody hell, I've lost them.' The inspector in Ryde said, 'Go and have a cup of tea and come back at 2.30 pm and a bus will take you to Pontin's Little Canada camp where your passengers will be having afternoon tea; you can catch up with them there. So we met up and they told me what a lovely day they had had, and that they were sorry I had missed it.

Several of my trips to Scotland gave me cause for alarm. I remember once feeling the old coach struggle as I was going up a hill with a very steep gradient. As I approached a right-hand bend a car came round at quite a pace with an elderly couple in it. Their faces were so shocked at seeing me; it must have looked like someone had built a brick wall across the road. The man steered away from the coach and straight up an embankment so that the car started to roll over across the road. I don't know what his intention could have been. I looked in my mirror as I passed the car and saw the door open and wondered whether he was going to jump out, but the door stuck in the tarmac and stopped the car from rolling.

I couldn't stop the bus as I would never have got it started again, but on reaching the top of the hill, some of the male passengers and I ran back to the car and helped the lady out. She had a right go at me, telling me I should not be on the road, but I think this was because they were both in shock. There was nothing we could do for the car, as the only thing stabilising it was the door in the tarmac.

We went back to the coach and I stopped in the first village to report what had happened and to get someone to rescue the couple and the car.

I had a similar experience when I was on my way to the Isle of Skye. The road was single-track with passing places and I had been pulling in regularly to let the cars behind me pass. This particular time I indicated to the car that I was going to pull over to let them pass, but as the driver went by he turned round and waved a thank-you to me. As he did so he drove straight into a ditch. I stopped and we jumped out to rescue the couple. Again I had to inform the police when we got to the nearest village. How did we ever manage without the cab phone?

Another story comes to mind of an overnight stop at the Station Hotel in Ayr, Scotland, where there were a few touring coaches also staying. We came down in the morning to load the luggage and found that one of the drivers was missing. He was a short, dumpy Scotsman who liked his wee dram. He drove for a well-known London tour company and had a party of American tourists on board.

We found out from the porters that he was still in bed and stoned out of his mind. So some of us drivers loaded his coach, while another went to his room to get him dressed, bring him down to his vehicle and sit him in the driver's seat. We said to him, 'All your passengers and luggage are aboard, so off you jolly well go.' We slapped him on the back and away he went.

I don't know what the Americans thought about it, but I never heard any more so he must have been all right.

I did meet some funny characters driving the coaches, and when a number of drivers got together some excelled themselves. I often got a few laughs myself. On one tour I put a coach blanket round my waist like a kilt and borrowed one of the ladies' handbags as a sporran for a joke; it seemed to go down very well with the ladies.

As the season came to an end, so did my time on the coaches. I felt a little sad about this as I had had a good run, but things have to move on. I was now thirty-three years old and Janne had just told me that I was to become a dad. I was over the moon. So Ian and I, with a couple of other drivers, applied for a job with Bowen's, the Esso Blue paraffin dealer for the north of London and were given a starting date for the winter months.

I had had a good life on the coaches, meeting some very interesting people and travelling the length and breadth of England, Scotland and Wales.

Coaching was in my blood, however, so I would later return to follow my father in doing casual weekend work.

Chapter 12

Regular Work

SO a group of us from the coaches began at Bowen, based in Barking. They had taken over an ex-Cleveland oil depot and used two eight-wheel Atkinsons, two Ford Thames Trader artics and a number of Thames Trader four-wheel tankers, which delivered paraffin all round north London. The eight-wheelers bridged into the terminal from Esso at Purfleet and the two artics delivered petrol to Bowen's garages.

We started there in quite a group, so we felt at home. We were put on paraffin deliveries straight away and were told about certain shops that we had to deliver to. I was given an oil shop and the regular drivers said, 'He always has two hundred gallons of blue, but his sight gauge is inaccurate and will register two hundred and fifty, so tell him you have put some extra in his tank and he will pay you for it.' I had to do this, otherwise it was bad for the regular drivers who did the deliveries all year. I carried out the delivery and told him the story and he said, 'Don't let my wife know I am on the fiddle,' and then he said, 'You boys do look after me.' Poor sod.

I had another delivery where the shop manager said, 'The tanks are in a shed in the back garden.' So I drove round the backs of the shops with my mate but when we looked in his tanks we saw they were full to the brim. We thought, 'What is he on, when did he last look at the tanks?' But we went through the motions, starting the engine and sitting in the cab revving for a while, and then we went in and told him the tanks were full; he signed our ticket and we left and sold it to the next customer.

I was in the yard another day when the manager called me to the office and said, 'Take my car to the stores and help Mr Bowen load his car and mine with stuff to take to Barking Town Hall.' As I walked away he shouted, 'And take Bill with you!'

I called Bill, another driver, and we went to the stores. The guv'nor there said, 'Put these boxes of oranges and apples in the cars and come back for these boxes of sweets.' So we loaded the cars and followed him to the Town Hall.

On the way Bill said, 'We'll have one of those boxes of sweets,' and put one under the seat.

When we got to the Town Hall, the guv'nor said, 'I suppose you're wondering what this is all about. Well, this is my contribution to the children's Christmas party.'

We started carrying the stuff in and I said to Bill, 'Get that box of sweets.'

But he said, 'No.'

'They are for the kids,' I said, 'you can't do that to them.' But he wouldn't listen.

When we finished taking the stuff in the guv'nor turned to us and said, 'Before you go, I'll just count those boxes of sweets.' Well, I have never seen anybody move as fast as Bill did that day; he came back puffing like an old man. The guv'nor was a tight old bastard, but I suppose that's how they make their money.

I used to deliver oil to his house in Shenfield where I would have to drive over his lawn. I would show him the dipstick and he would shout, 'Hand it down! I cannot see it up there.' So I would hand him the stick and watch the oil run down his arm. He would then insist on seeing the dry dip so he could examine the bottom of the stick to see if it was wet.

I happened to mention this some time later at one of his local garages when I took a petrol tanker over there and the manager told me a similar story about him. 'He has all his groceries delivered here,' he said, 'and I run them to his home. On one occasion I had to pull up sharp and the box of groceries fell on the floor, so I stopped and picked them up and carried on to his house. On the way back I heard something rolling about on the floor, so I stopped, found an apple, and ate it.

'When I got back to the garage the phone was ringing and it was the guv'nor. He said, "have you eaten one of my apples? I weighed them and it was short weight." I explained what had happened and he said, "Well, that's all right then."'

In early December, Bowen decided to buy two old Esso eight-wheel tankers, an AEC Mammoth Major Mk 3 and a Leyland Octopus for bridging between the Esso in Purfleet and our depot in Barking. Bridging involved moving the oil between terminals and unloading it so that the smaller vehicles could deliver it. I volunteered with another driver to do the work, as I didn't like running round oil shops with cans of paraffin, whereas the other drivers didn't like doing bridging because they couldn't earn so much money from all the tips and the fiddling.

I took over the AEC and we loaded it up with diesel, heating oil and paraffin and bridged it back to the Barking depot, pumping it into our storage tanks so that the smaller tankers could load from there. The two Atkinsons were doing more petrol deliveries so we had to do their work too.

My father's birthday was on 3rd January and he was insisting that Janne had the baby on that date. January was fast approaching and on the 4th our baby daughter was born and we named her Angela. My parents were over the moon, as were Janne and I. This was my parents' second grandchild as my sister had a boy who was now two and a half.

Bowen was negotiating with Esso for a new contract, so in the meantime we started loading out of Mobil Oil at Coryton near Stanford-le-Hope. Distillate oil was sent from there by rail to the large Nechells gasworks in Birmingham. The train would shunt the trucks into the gasworks, where there was a large delivery pipe with a flexible hose coming out of it to couple to the outlet pipe of the truck tanks.

There was quite a problem there in January 1966; it made it into all the papers. Nine rail trucks each carrying 8,000 gallons of distillate were shunting into the works. Apparently one of the trucks was leaking. A workman walking past with a hurricane lamp accidentally ignited the distillate vapour. They said afterwards that he was a lucky to be alive.

This started one of the biggest fires ever seen in Birmingham. The heat was so intense that it melted the front of one of the fire engines.

This then became a case of national emergency because, without the oil, the Birmingham gasworks would have had to shut down, cutting off thousands of homes and businesses. Mobil asked Bowen if they could send three eight-wheelers to their Coventry depot and base them there, so that they could rail the distillate to that depot and the three tankers could then bridge it to the gasworks.

Volunteers were called for so I offered to go, along with two other drivers. One of these was the son-in-law of Charlie Howard, the coach driver I had been following from Jedburgh when I had my accident; his name was Mark. We were sent home to get some things and then we took the two Atkinsons and the Leyland Octopus up to the Mobil terminal in Coventry. Mark and I, who had become quite good pals, took the Atkinsons while the other driver took the Leyland. He was a bit upset to have the older vehicle, though I don't know why. The Atkinsons would do thirty-five miles per hour with the Gardner 150 engine, but would struggle on hills. Instead, the Leyland Octopus did thirty miles per hour up hill and down dale, so although we were all right on the flat, he would catch us on the hills.

We parked the motors in the Coventry terminal and were taken to a guest house where the Mobil staff had arranged for us to stay. The next morning we started loading and bridging to the gas works. When we arrived I could not believe my eyes, the rail tankers had become just a heap of metal; the heat generated must have been colossal, because nobody would ever have imagined that they used to be railway trucks.

A young boy said to us, 'Go and have a cup of tea and I'll unload your motors,' and some time later he came in to tell us we were ready to go.

When we arrived back at Coventry I pulled on the loading rack and walked up the gantry to stand on the tank top and load the motor for another run. As I got there I looked in amazement as the boy had left one lid open with half a full pot. I thought, 'What if I had driven off and a cigarette had been thrown out of a bus window as I was passing it?' I was especially worried after seeing what had happened to the rail trucks.

When I returned to the gas works I had a go at the boy, but his answer was, 'You are the driver, you should have checked.' So I told him not to go near my vehicle again and I would unload it, the same went for the other two drivers.

Coventry terminal was one of a kind; petrol flowed like water. The cars were parked in the terminal opposite the loading bays and every week all the cars in the terminal were filled to the brim. They had a spotlessly clean dustbin for petrol during the week if needed. I had never been in a terminal as good as this one. Every Saturday one of the drivers came in with meat to sell, another would bring fish and someone else would bring clothing; it was like a mini market.

It was also a lovely area. Mark and I used to race one another along the road in the Akkos and sometimes his foot would come out of the driver's door window doing circular motions indicating me to overtake. I would pull alongside him and he would push his arm out to point at the surrounding country side and shout, 'Look o'er the Dales!' He was a right star turn and had the looks to go with it; the girls loved him.

We were informed by Bowen that we had relief drivers coming up on Monday and so we could go home on Saturday. We trained it home and then after a week we would come back. Mark and I used to leave home and meet at Toddington on the M1 at midnight and have something to eat, getting to Coventry for a 6 o'clock start.

One weekend I was running short of petrol and Mark said that if I could make it to the terminal I could get some there rather than buying it. We arrived at the terminal and Mark said, 'Look, Paddy is in the loading bay, ask him for some petrol.' Paddy was an Irish Mobil driver; I walked up to him and said, 'Paddy, can I have some juice?'

He said, 'Oy, go and get the dustbin.' So I found the bin and stood between the gantry and the tanker and held the dustbin stretched fully out. I don't think it occurred to me what the weight would be like, but I never had time to find out. Paddy swung the loading arm across into the bin and hit the loading button, but the petrol hit the bottom of the bin with such force that it took it straight out of my hands and sent it flying across the terminal. I stood there with petrol pouring over me, completely blinded and staggering about. My so-called mates stood looking at me and couldn't stop laughing, but they eventually grabbed me, undressed me and put me in the showers. They also found me some clean overalls to wear.

The office wanted to know how I came to be soaked in petrol. I told them, 'I was just talking to the driver and the arm shot out.' So they had the bay tested and everybody loading on that bay was told to be very careful. I couldn't tell them what really happened, although I think they had a good idea because their cars were filled every Saturday as well. They said that it must have been an act of god. 'Oh, nice one,' I thought.

When I went to get my clothes from the dry cleaners where my mates had taken them the staff said, 'We all stood outside while the clothes were being cleaned, in case the place blew up!'

If the gas works did not want any oil, Mobil sent us out with their vehicles delivering petrol all around the

Midlands. I really liked this, so much so that I thought about moving up to Coventry.

Sometimes when they were busy they got the fitter to go out on deliveries. He had a little pump which he used to take the petrol straight from the storage tank onto his road tanker, bypassing the loading rack and meters. One day they stopped him at the gate to do a spot check and he said, 'I haven't got time to waste, do you want this load delivered or not? Make up your mind.' So rather than upsetting him they let him go and he gave a sigh of relief.

One day one of the Mobil drivers asked me if they checked the dips at the gas works and I said no, so he said, 'Leave two hundred gallons off and I will load it on my vehicle.' We did this and that night he paid me my share and said, 'Are we all right for tomorrow?' and I said, 'Let my mates have a go.' We did this change-over for about six weeks and then another contractor took over so we came back home. I found out later that the new contractors were caught doing the shortages and were fined for stealing.

A few years later Mark started a mini-cab business and asked me if I wanted some weekend work. I started doing a bit but I quickly realised that it was mostly picking up drunks from the pubs in the late evenings. I thought, 'This is not for me,' and got out before I had anyone throw up in the car.

A good friend of mine, Ron, had come to Bowen with me from the seasonal coaches, and we always worked together when we could. One Saturday Ron was out delivering with a regular Bowen driver and didn't get back to the terminal until late and, as everyone normally finished early on a Saturday, the place was fairly empty.

As they pulled up at the terminal, Ron volunteered to bunker the tanker while the regular driver went to the office to fill in the sheets and put the money in the safe. Having bunkered and parked up, Ron made his way to the office to find the other driver, where he was met by a masked man pointing a shotgun at him. The other driver and the night watchman were lying tied up on the floor, where another robber was pointing a gun at them. Before he had time to think, Ron was tied up as well and the masked men were demanding that they gave them the safe combination. The drivers and the watchman looked at them blankly and tried to explain that they didn't know what it was, only the office staff did.

Apparently these rogues had been watching the terminal for a while and knew that all the drivers and staff should have been finished up by that time on a Saturday, but it just so happened that on that particular day Ron and the other driver had been late. The only money available was what they had collected that day and so the gunmen left empty-handed.

Once they were left alone, they managed to free themselves and call the police. They were all very shaken by the experience, but they were taken to Barking police station for interviews and statements. Once there Ron asked if he could phone his wife, as she would be worrying as to why he was so late. He got through to her and told her that he had been involved in a hold-up and that he would be home soon. 'A likely story!' she said, 'I know you've been down the pub with your mates!' He had a hell of a job convincing her.

Ron said afterwards that he had been shitting himself in that office as the men tried to crack the safe open. He said he did not want to look down the barrel of a shotgun ever again.

Time was fast approaching for the summer season to start and I had to make a decision soon about what I was going to do, but luckily it was made for me. One of the drivers on the Thames Trader artic who delivered petrol to Bowen's petrol stations decided to leave, so I asked the manager if I could take over his regular job and he said yes. It was my first regular job for some time.

I felt a little sad as I said my goodbyes to Ian and the other drivers who were returning for another season on the coaches, as we had been like a band of brothers. But Janne had never been happy about me being on the coaches, and when I look back now it was a good thing I packed up and got a job with a pension.

I took over the Thames Trader artic, which pulled an ex-Esso tank of 2,000 gallons, divided into four 500-gallon compartments. When it was loaded with the lids shut the petrol showed an inch above the 500 gallon mark on the dipstick. I made a lot of money with this tank.

I remember explaining to a garage owner once that I had bought a Commer minibus with twelve seats, to take the family out on trips, and I wanted to know how much four remould tyres would cost me. He said, 'You can't put remoulds on if you are carrying people. Bring the motor to me and I will put four new tyres and tubes on it and you can pay me as and when you can.'

'Are you joking?'

'No,' he said.

I used to deliver to him twice a week and always told him that I had twenty gallons extra for him, which he gave me half a crown a gallon for, so I collected £5 altogether. He also always gave me a £2 tip, so I would get £7 a load. I decided to take my minibus to him and so he put the tyres and tubes on for me. When I delivered to him I would tell him to take that money off my bill, so in actual fact the tyres and tubes cost me nothing and he got nothing. As I write this I think, 'what a trick to pull', but I feel very guilty.

On one occasion after I had loaded up at Esso, I pulled out and approached the traffic lights at Stonehouse corner. The light was green and I saw a van coming towards me, but I also saw a young girl, who had been standing on the kerb, suddenly run across the road. As she did so the van hit her and knocked her across the road and under the front of me. Luckily I was on a gradual incline and had foreseen what might happen so was not travelling at great speed; nevertheless she was under the motor and an ambulance was called. We tried to make her as comfortable as possible, but she was crying a lot, probably more from the shock than the injuries. She was taken away quickly by the ambulance. I had to see the police to give them a statement, but I never heard any more about it.

In August 1966 my father was taken ill and diagnosed with cancer; he was given six months to live and died on the 30th September, at 56 years old, when Angela was only nine months. I was sorry that she was not old enough to remember him because he would have been a great granddad to her; he pushed her in the pram whenever he had the opportunity and was so proud of her. I know he would still be very proud of her now that she is grown up; she is very much like him, always enjoying life. He had so wanted to be there for her first birthday to share this as well.

I was heartbroken; I had lost a father whom I loved dearly, who had taught me all I knew, all about driving for a living and who I think was proud of my achievements as a driver. He was both my father and my mate and we spent many trips together on the coaches at weekends. I will never forget him.

I used to deliver to a garage that belonged to Bowen. It was an Esso site, at Gallows Corner, Romford, but they had a couple of Bowen's pumps. I would deliver to the same garage, with the same load, into the same underground tank, and it would feed into two pumps, one Esso Extra, and the other Bowen, which was sixpence a gallon cheaper than the Esso pump. But you try telling the customer it was the same, they would not have it.

Just before I left Bowen I was loading in Esso and the terminal supervisor came up to me and said, 'I want to do a spot check on you,' and proceeded to check the dips in the compartments. He said, 'Oh, oh, oh, what have we here? Have you been a bad boy, then? Go and get the drip cans.' So I found the cans and he lifted the foot valve to let petrol down the line to the outlet pipe and then shut it. He told me to drain the line into the can and he then opened the lid and re-dipped the compartment and found I was short on the dipstick. He said, 'How much have you drained off?'

I replied, 'Only what you let down the line.'

So he said, 'Well, give it back to me,' and he replaced it in the compartment. He looked puzzled and dipped it again; it was right on the line so he just turned to me and said, 'Clear off.'

I was delivering to a garage in Ilford once when a lady driver came into the garage with a Jaguar car and pulled up behind the tanker. After filling with petrol she asked me to move the tanker so she could leave the garage. I explained that I was unloading petrol so she would have to reverse out and she said, 'I can't reverse the car.'

So I said, 'Well why did you pull in behind me, then? You could have gone the other side of the pumps!'

'There was a car there.'

'Well, you could have waited for them to go.' She went on to say that she was in a hurry and could I reverse the car out for her. I said, 'No, I'm not insured to drive your car,' but the petrol pump attendant said he would do it. I said to him afterwards, 'She shouldn't be on the road if she can't reverse the car.'

Once, when I had just finished loading in Esso I was getting off the gantry and saw some loading staff playing football, or so I thought. One of the lads called to me to kick the ball back to them as it was coming my way. I ran towards the ball and gave it an almighty kick. My foot stopped dead on impact and I spun round backwards like a top, nearly drilling a hole in the ground, in fact I nearly broke my foot. All of the staff were falling about laughing like mad.

It turned out that the ball was in fact what they call the 'pig', which was solid rubber and was used to separate the fuels as it pumped through the oil pipes lines. I was not amused and told them so. They apologised and said, 'We thought you knew it was the pig.'

We spent a lot of time when loading out of Esso in the Noak café. When ordering breakfast there you had the full English with a fried slice but only paid for the set breakfast at first. Then when your breakfast came up he would ask for the money for the fried slice as he was always frightened that someone who had only ordered a full English would take the one with the fried slice without paying for it.

One Saturday three of us loaded up and headed for the Noak. When we arrived the café was empty apart from us and he was very pleased to see us as he was having some renovation work done at the rear of the café and the builders wanted a large lintel lifted in place, so he asked if we could help. We went round to the side of the café where the two builders told us what had to be done and so the five of us struggled to lift the lintel and put it in its place.

He thanked us and we went into the café and ordered our breakfast. We still had to pay for our tea, though; what a tight bastard!

It was around this time that I decided to find a job with a major oil company.

While I was at Bowen's I got friendly with one of the drivers named Jim who had a Ford Thames van which he had converted it to a camper van. When he found out that I had bought a Commer twelve-seater he wanted me to do the same, but I said, 'If I wanted a camper, I would have got one.'

He insisted that I converted it, however, and told me I could still have twelve seats but we could also have week-ends away. He convinced me, so I went round his house a couple of times and he helped me to take all the seats out and convert it to a camper van.

My mother bought us a camping stove, which meant we could always stop for a cuppa, so I took a single seat out on the nearside rear of the van and made a small cabinet for it.

One of my favourite recollections of the camper van was when we were away with Jim and his family in Cornwall and he wanted us all to go to an air display at a local airbase. We arrived at the airbase and were directed to the make-shift car park and got out to watch the displays.

During this time Jim and I wanted the toilet so we asked

an airman where the piss-hole was and he directed us to a large building.

As we approached it we were stopped by military police who wanted to know why we were near a restricted area and a top-security building. We told them that we were here for the air display and they said, 'What air display?' and then we had one hell of a job convincing them there was an air display going on and that we were told the *piss-hole* was in this building.

They started laughing after this and said, 'Someone is having you on, they probably thought you meant the C.O.' They didn't take any chances with us, however, and escorted us to the toilets, even standing there while we used it, and then escorting us away from the building.

We arrived back to the vans to find that Jim's had an oil leak, so Janne and Jim's wife Joyce started making sandwiches and tea, while Jim and I found the service station at the camp and bought some oil. We were lying under the van, looking for the oil leak while the wives and children sat in the van having their meals, when we heard a voice saying, 'Are you going to be long?'

We crawled out to see two airmen sitting in a Land Rover and they repeated, 'Are you going to be long? We want to open the runway up.' We looked round and saw that we were the only two vehicles left and that we were in the middle of one of the runways which had used for the car park. We made a hasty retreat and could not stop laughing at the trouble we had caused. Well, we were on holiday.

Chapter 13

Starting at Gulf

THE year was 1967, I was 34 years old and I had been at Bowen's for about two years. Angela was twelve months old and Janne was pregnant with our second child, which was due in April 1968.

I was starting to think about which major oil companies I should try for a job, though I knew it would be a hard struggle because drivers who got into the majors never left until they died.

When I was on tour with the coaches I had once got quite pally with two male passengers and we used to have a drink together in the evenings at the hotels. They told me that they drove for Samuel Williams at Dagenham Dock and would put in a good word for me if I ever wanted a job there at the end of the season. The job was such a good one that it went on recommendation and was handed from father to son. Sammy Williams had been on contract to Gulf Oil delivering gas and fuel oils. Gulf had wanted the lorries painted in their logo, but Williams had declined, so they eventually lost the contract. As a result, some of the drivers had traded over to Gulf.

So I decided to try Gulf Oil at Dagenham Dock. I drove there in my car and went into the office. A man was sitting at his desk so I asked him, 'Have you any driving vacancies?'

He looked at me: 'How old are you?'

'Thirty-four.'

'That's OK then,' he said, 'because if you are older than that you can't be in the pension scheme,' and he proceeded to give me some application forms. I filled them in then and there to save coming back again.

I went home thinking 'Well, they didn't chuck me out and tell me that they never have any vacancies. So maybe I have a chance.'

A few days later I had a phone call from the manager who said, 'I want you to come here for a driving test.' He suggested Friday at 4.30 pm. I arrived at 4.20 pm and went to see the manager who said, 'The driving instructor will be along shortly.' So I waited and a man came in. I heard some arguing in the manager's office but I took no notice. The man came out of the office with a briefcase and said, 'Mr Heymer?' I followed him out into the tanker park where a Guy Invincible artic stood. The sky was dark and it was pouring with rain, but he said, 'Get in and we will go for a little ride.'

I jumped in, started the motor and found the windscreen wipers. The vehicle was all strange to me and filthy; I had a job to see out the windscreen. Anyway, he took me all round Ilford and Barking and eventually said, 'I want you to pull over at the off-side of the road and back into that turning. I thought, 'This is dangerous.' It was peak time and I was going to reverse with the oncoming traffic, but I did it and he said, 'OK, now pull out and I want you to back in on your blind side.' Now I was going to reverse against the traffic. I started reversing and watching the traffic coming up behind me. I managed to get in so far, then stopped and pulled forward to straighten up for another shunt; I assumed he wanted the motor right on the corner. He said, 'No, try again.' I had to do it again and again, and the more tries I had the worse it was getting. He gave it up as a bad job and said, 'Let's get back to the depot.'

We arrived back and the manager was waiting and said, 'How was this driver?' The instructor told him that he had failed me and the manager said, 'What did you fail him on?'

'He had to make a shunt backing in on his blind side.'

'Is that bad?' the manager asked.

'We like them to do it in one go,' the instructor replied.

'Well, I want this driver to pass, so I want him to do a re-test tomorrow.'

The instructor said, 'That's OK, but it will have to be with another instructor.'

One of the regular drivers came in, a veteran tanker driver of many years, and the manager said, 'Snuffy, do you want an hour's overtime?'

The driver looked suspicious: 'Doing what?'

'Take this driver down the yard,' replied the manager, 'and do some reversing on his blind side.' We went down the yard and put some forty gallon barrels out for me to reverse round. Snuffy was so-called because he took snuff; he later became something of a father figure to me. He was an ex-Crow Carrying driver.

He asked me what this was all about and I told him. I said I wasn't really interested in the job now, anyway.

Snuffy cheered me up, though: 'I've driven tankers for thirty years,' he said, 'and even I have to make a shunt now and again. You should have got out and said, "You show me how it is done, then!" Don't get depressed, go for the test tomorrow and good luck.'

I found out later that I had been the third driver to take

the test and that the driver who had gone before me hit a car in Ilford and didn't stop. That was what the row had been about while I waited outside the office. The instructor had been panicking because the driver kept denying that he had in fact hit the car. I met up with this driver much later when he was working for another oil company and he said, 'You were the driver who took the test after me?'

I said, 'I don't know, I didn't see anybody.' He went on to say that he did in fact hit the car, but made out to the instructor that he hadn't and started laughing. 'Sod them,' he said.

The following morning at 10 o'clock I arrived at the depot and saw a young-looking man with a briefcase who said, 'Mr Heymer, let's do it.' We went out to the tanker park and found the same vehicle and proceeded to drive round Barking and Ilford. At last he said, 'We will do the reversing now.'

So I backed in on my side, pulled out and started to back in on my blind side and stopped. He said, 'What have you stopped for?' I told him that I was going to straighten up, but he said, 'I don't care how far back you go into this road, as long as it finishes up parallel to the kerb.'

So I carried on reversing and stopped, then he said, 'That didn't hurt, did it? Get out now, it's my turn to drive; I like to keep my hand in.'

We changed places and I said, 'What about me?'

'What about you? You've passed.' So we drove back to the terminal.

Both of my instructors had been from the British School of Motoring at East Ham. The second one told me that the instructor I had had the day before was so wound up with the previous driver hitting the car that he lost his cool. He also said that he had been a tipper driver before becoming an instructor. 'That figures,' I thought.

I was offered a seasonal job for the rest of the winter, the manager saying that he only gave full-time jobs to drivers who were already part-time there, not ones who came in off the street. So I decided to take a chance. 'Maybe if it doesn't work out I can go back coaching,' I thought, though this seemed very unlikely.

The depot manager said, 'When can you start?'

'I'll have to give notice to my employer, so I can start in one week's time.'

'Great,' he said, 'I'll send you a formal letter of employment, starting Monday week.'

However, on the Saturday morning I had a phone call from the manager asking again if I was still OK for the Monday, which I said yes to.

Then he said, 'I don't like to throw this at you, but I desperately need an extra driver for nights. As we work in shifts, you'll have to start on the night shift. Is that all right?'

I agreed to start at 10 pm on Monday and was left to wonder what working nights would be like.

On Monday evening I said goodbye and 'see you in the morning' to Janne and drove to Dagenham. I walked into the office at 9.45 pm to be met by the traffic clerk who said, 'You must be the new driver. We've got no work for you, but when the other two drivers come in we will sort you out with overalls and a donkey jacket.'

The two drivers arrived and I was issued with the working gear and told to come back tomorrow night at the same time. Puzzled, I asked, 'Do I get paid?' and was assured I would be.

As time went on I found out that the drivers always

volunteered for nights because there was never much work and it was like having a week's holiday. I arrived back home that night at 11.15 to find Janne in bed. 'What are you doing home?' she asked.

'I've chucked the job in,' I replied.'

The response came quickly: 'But you've only been there five minutes!' So I went on to explain what had happened. I thought it was strange as the manager had said he was desperate for night drivers.

I returned every night and the same thing kept happening, until Friday when we were each given a load. I had to take a load of gas oil to Kings Cross where a small oil distributor was based. I found the place all right, as well as the gas oil tank connection and made the delivery.

I arrived back at the terminal where the other two drivers were waiting for me with a cup of tea. They asked if everything had gone to plan and I said yes. At that moment the phone rang, one of the drivers answered it and said to me, 'You have just come through the main gate and the security officer said that your fire extinguisher fell off the trailer and shot straight into their office. They thought it was a bomb! They want you to go and get it and fill out an incident form.' So I went down to their hut, made out the form and picked up the extinguisher. What an odd first week.

There was more to come, however. On Monday morning I started on day work. I was told that I had over-filled the tank on the Friday night, but that it wasn't my fault as the load had been sent a day early; I had not known because the tank I was pumping into was at the back of other tanks. I then met some more of the drivers and after being given a load I followed one of them to Thames Haven.

I had a four-wheel Albion and the other driver had an AEC Mandator artic which he did not drive over thirty miles per hour. 'He's a bit of a plodder,' I thought.

When we got to the terminal, he asked, 'I wasn't going too fast for you, was I?'

'No, it was fine.'

'I was going flat out.' I thought he was joking, but he wasn't.

Gulf had an assortment of vehicles, from the four-wheel Albion, the eight-wheel Scammell, Scammell Highwayman artic, six-wheel Leyland Constructor, AEC Mandators and Mercurys, Guy Invincibles, Leyland Beaver artics and Volvos. The tanks were straight and belly ones (the same as Mobil), with twin, single-axle and four-in-line trailers.

I had been at Gulf a few weeks when my turn to do nights came round again. I went through the same procedure of having nothing to do until Friday night, when there was only one load to take to a garage in Old Kent Road. One of the drivers volunteered to do it, but we said we would go along for the ride. We got to the garage and while the driver made the delivery we sat talking to the garage manager in his office. A short time later the driver came in looking worried and said he had dropped the diesel down the petrol tank. The driver sitting with me said, 'Let's get the diesel back out and then on Monday they will deliver another load, so the garage will not lose any customers.'

The garage manager lent the drivers his Land Rover so they both went back to the depot to get searcher pipes and extra hoses and left me sitting on the top of the road tanker with the garage forecourt pump hose, drawing up the diesel and petrol mix from the underground tank. I had been sitting on the top of the tank for about an hour

and a half when they came back and we immediately
changed the hoses over on the cargo pump so that it would
suck the fuel out of the underground tank into the road
tanker.

After some time, and a lot of priming, it started to come
up, the only trouble was that the engine was racing away.
It was after midnight and there were flats at the back of the
garage, so the police soon arrived and wanted to know
what the noise was all about as the flats were complaining.
The drivers explained and the police said, 'Be as quick as
you can.' So we were as quick as could be and left at
7 o'clock in the morning; the motor had been running flat
out all night.

We got back to the depot and informed the office clerk
and he arranged to send another load. Some of the other
drivers found out that our tanker was loaded and started
draining it off, only to get half-way down the road in their
cars before they conked out, not realising it was a mixed
load. The load had to go back into the storage tanks to be
downgraded.

On Monday morning I was the first to be summoned to
see the depot manager, who wanted my account of what
had taken place. I told him exactly what had happened, but
left out that we had used the cargo pump, as it is illegal to
pump petrol through that, but as I was the junior driver I
had had no say in what they had done. He said to me, 'Did
you at any time use the cargo pump?' I denied we had and
he said, 'I believe you are lying.'

So I explained again what we did and that we got the
fuel out with the pump. He snapped then and said, 'What
pump?' Again I said, 'The petrol pump in the garage.'

He said that there were 1,500 gallons to be pumped out
and, taking the average time at something or other at a rate

of so many gallons per minute, it would take this amount of time, so I wouldn't be finished until 7 am.

'That's right,' I said. 'That's why we didn't get back until a quarter past eight.'

He dismissed me, saying: 'I'm not finished with you yet.'

My main priority then was to see the other drivers before the guv'nor did, to warn them. I managed to see the driver who made the mistake and he said, 'I'll give the same version as you,' but when I saw the driver who had been in the office with me, he said, 'I'll tell him the truth.'

'You can't do that,' I said, 'we will all be in the shit.' But he went ahead and told the guv'nor and he had us all in the office straight away. He looked directly at me and said, 'I knew you were lying and I have a good mind to sack the three of you.' Still looking at me, he said, 'I know you were covering for the other two, now get out of my office.'

I made a hasty retreat and when I spoke later to the two drivers they said he gave them a right rollicking and blamed them for leading me astray.

I started at 6 o'clock at Dagenham one morning and had to load at Purfleet for a delivery to a garage in Basingstoke. There was a queue waiting to load when I got there, but when I eventually did get loaded I found I had a puncture. I phoned the office and was told that someone would come to me, so I waited for the tyre repair team to arrive. They came with another driver to take over my vehicle because I was running so late, and he would give me a lift back to the terminal as he passed by.

We got the tyre repaired and left the depot to make our way back. The driver pulled up at the café for breakfast but I said, 'I've got to get back to the terminal.'

He said, 'Have you had your breakfast yet?' I hadn't, so he said, 'You've got to eat, so have it now.'

I was panicking, but we had our meal and left. When we got to Choates Road by the Chequers pub he stopped to let me out and said, 'You can walk down to the depot from here.'

It was about three-quarters of a mile and I ran all the way. When I got to the outer office I sat down and said to the other drivers, 'If he asks, tell him I've been here for ages.'

The supervisor looked out of the window and saw me. 'Come here,' he said.

I thought, 'This is it, he's going to give me a rollocking.'

But I was wrong: 'I want you to get a lift to Barking,' he said, 'and collect a motor from the paint shop.'

So I walked outside and waited for a tanker to leave the depot. One soon arrived and he dropped me off at Barking. I had a mile to walk and when I got there the vehicle was still not ready so I had to wait. When it was ready for release I got half-way back but then had to park up for a night out as my time was up. I got a lift home and took the motor back the next morning. I fully expected the supervisor to say, 'What's this? You'll be bloody lucky!' to my night-out request, but nothing was said.

On 2nd April 1968 to our delight, our second daughter was born, at Forest Gate maternity hospital. We named her Lee-Anne.

I always enjoyed calling in at home whenever I could. One day when I popped home for a cuppa, Janne looked out of our upstairs window to see a policeman with a Noddy bike looking at my motor. I rushed downstairs: 'Are you looking for me, officer?'

'Is this your vehicle? We've had a complaint about it.'

'Well, I'm going shortly. I only called in for a cuppa.'

'Don't be too long, then,' he finished.

A couple of days later a neighbour knocked on the door. 'There's lots of petrol running out of your tanker,' he said.

'Well, grab a can fast,' I replied, walking to the motor with him in tow.

I bent down under the back of the tank and put my hands in the contents and said to him, 'Smell that.'

'I can't smell anything.'

'I know you can't. That's because it's rainwater running from the tank top and down the tank drain holes. I don't carry petrol, only black oil. You were the one who phoned the police the other day, weren't you?'

He denied it, and I sighed: 'The trouble is, you automatically think of petrol when you see a tanker.'

In June the supervisor told me that as I had served my six-month probation period and they had lost two drivers, he could now offer me a permanent job. I would receive a letter in the post to state this fact. He also told me that they were moving to Purfleet depot in the near future. 'I don't believe it,' I thought. 'I didn't go to EP because they were moving to Purfleet.'

I always remember that supervisor; he was never flustered. One day when I told him I didn't have time to do a particular delivery, he took the delivery notes and threw them on the desk. 'What don't go today will go tomorrow,' he said. 'You won't give me ulcers.'

I was delivering to a garage in Richmond once and was having a cup of tea in the garage kiosk with the pump attendant when there was an almighty crash outside on the forecourt. We both dashed out to see that a mini had driven down the manhole.

The front offside wheel was in the manhole, resting on the delivery hose and the rear nearside wheel was in the air.

The woman passenger was holding on to the steering wheel to steady herself as the car leaned over and the driver was standing at the back of the car whistling, quite unaware of the car in the manhole.

'That's clever,' I said, pointing to the car and when he looked he stood back in amazement. 'Didn't you know you had driven into the hole?' I added.

He shook his head: 'I was looking back out of the window to see what pump I wanted and never noticed a thing.'

We went round to the back of the garage and got all the fitters to help us lift the car out.

I was given a Guy Invincible artic and after some time I had differential trouble in the back axle and a new differential was installed. At first I didn't notice any difference but then I began to think all was not right. The speedo said I was doing a certain speed but I was sure it was different.

One day when there were two of us on the same delivery I said to my mate, 'I will do thirty miles per hour and you follow me and tell me what your speedo says.' After a while we stopped and he told me I was only doing twenty miles per hour. 'Well, I'll do forty now,' I said, 'and you see what that is.' We stopped again and he said I was doing thirty.

When we got back I told the fleet engineer. They did tests and found that they had put the wrong ratio diff in and it had to come out and be replaced. The motor did pull well – I thought it had a new lease of life.

I was out with another driver once who said, 'On the way home we'll stop on the motorway and do some scrumping.'

I followed him until he stopped on the hard shoulder. 'We can't stop here,' I exclaimed.

He laughed: 'Don't worry.' He then tied the legs of his boiler suit together, climbed the embankment, hopped over a fence and disappeared. I thought we were both going to get nicked, two tankers parked up like we were, so I lifted the engine cowling in the cab just in case.

After a while he came back with his overalls filled with apples. 'Try these for size,' he said and emptied half into the nearside of the cab, throwing one to me. As we left I took one bite and threw it away; it was sour. When we got back he said, 'What do you think?'

I didn't like to say what I really thought, so I replied, 'Lovely.'

He came up to me some time later: 'You prat,' he laughed. 'They were horrible. I threw them all away.'

'Well, after all your work I didn't want to dishearten you.'

Gulf moved to a depot in Grays, Essex shortly after that and we were offered a flat in Aveley. Soon after we moved there one of the drivers left his vehicle on an incline facing the offices and used the dead-man brake instead of the main handbrake (the dead-man brake was just a trailer brake) while he collected his loading notes and suddenly there was an almighty bang. It turned out that the vehicle had an air leak so when the air tank was exhausted it released the brakes and the vehicle went into the office block toilets causing excessive damage. It was a good thing nobody was sitting in there.

I saw this happen another time but on this occasion one of the drivers tried to stop it by climbing into the cab as it was moving, putting his foot on the revolving wheel. I could see he was going to be trapped between the vehicle and the wall so I shouted to him, 'Let it go!' He jumped out of the way just in time as it hit the office toilet block once more.

Another time I was standing with some drivers at the ticket office waiting for our loading meter tickets, laughing and joking, when there was a loud bang. A driver walked round to where we were standing and said, 'Who has that nice, shiny, newly painted tanker?' A driver looked up and quite proudly stated that he did. The first driver said, 'Well, it's just gone through the shit house.' We all ran round to find that this really had happened as he also had not applied the main handbrake.

They ended up repairing the toilets so many times that we were banned from parking in front of the offices; though the staff were too frightened to use them anyway.

Some of the tankers were well past their sell-by date, so you would have to map a route out to miss some of the larger hills. I remember once getting to Canning Town traffic lights and missing a number of green lights because every time I tried to start off, the unit kept bucking and rearing up, flinging dust into the cab. I couldn't get it to pull away and it was holding up all the traffic behind me. You just had to hope that when you reached the lights they would be in your favour, or hang back and at the right time go for it.

A group of us were standing in the yard one day chatting when one of our vehicles pulled in. When we saw the two drivers get out we all fell about laughing; they were both covered in white powder and looked like the McDougall's flour graders, one driver even had a beard so he looked like Father Christmas; what a sight. Apparently the driver riding shotgun put his feet up on top of the fire

extinguisher in the cab and it went off, covering everything with white powder. The whole terminal was in
uproar at the sight of these two and I wondered what
people would have thought as they drove along the road
looking like two white ghosts driving a tanker.

I had the four-wheel tanker for a day once and had to
load two hundred gallons of regular petrol, two hundred
gallons of premium petrol and eight hundred gallons of
diesel. The operator said that the premium meter wasn't
working so I would have to load on the dipstick, which I
did. When I had finished loading the operator said, 'I will
check your load now. How have you loaded it?'

'Two hundred gallons of regular in the number one
compartment, two hundred gallons of premium in the
number two compartment and three hundred and five
hundred gallons of diesel in four and five.' He checked the
dips and signed my loading note. As I started to pull out of
the bay the supervisor came running out and stopped me,
saying he wanted to do a spot check. I told him how I was
loaded, too, and after checking the load he signed my
ticket.

I left the terminal and on my way to the garage I kept
thinking about how I was loaded and suddenly I realised I
had loaded three hundred gallons of premium instead of
two hundred. It was only a small garage I was going to and
they catered mainly for London taxis. I approached the
guv'nor there and asked him if he could take the extra
hundred gallons but his tanks were only small so he
couldn't. I didn't know where to flog it so I had no
alternative but to return it to the terminal. I phoned my
manager and told him that I had one hundred gallons too
much and he said, 'You'll have to bring it back then, won't
you?'

When I got back all hell broke loose as both the operator and the supervisor had checked the load and nobody
had realised that I had a hundred gallons extra on board. I
suggested that maybe they had set me up to see what I
would do when I found out I had the extra gallons, but
they were going to sack both of them and turn my name to
mud for not getting rid of it.

The customs officers often carried out spot checks and I
got to know one of them quite well. I asked him what
would happen if I were caught with extra if it was a genuine
mistake. 'We have a pretty good idea if it's genuine or
stealing,' he replied.

'Yes, I bet,' I thought. 'Everybody in their eyes is
guilty.'

I was always fooling about at the depot, making out I
had tripped up the kerb by putting my right foot behind
my left and stumbling. I was on the loading bay once when
I saw John, one of the fitters, walking towards the workshop, so I ran down the gantry steps calling his name and
walking quite fast across the terminal to meet him through
the pouring rain. He looked round to see who was calling
and when I saw him looking at me I did my party trick,
only this time it went wrong. I had put my right foot
behind my left as though to trip, but my right foot stayed
behind my left and I went smack down on my face in the
wet yard.

I jumped up hoping he had not seen me, but he had,
and stood laughing his head off and requesting a replay. I
felt such a wally and was soaked all down my front; from
then on John kept telling everybody to get Al to trip up.

I was told to take a vehicle to the Gulf depot in
Silvertown one afternoon and that the fleet engineer
would be there to look over the motor. I drove into the

workshop and two men in brown smock coats were there. I had never met the fleet engineer before, so I started talking to the one I thought he was, telling him all that I thought was wrong with the vehicle. I arrived back to Purfleet and the supervisor called me to the office and said, 'Have you met the fleet engineer before?'

I said I hadn't and he said, 'I thought not, you were talking to the Ministry of Transport engineer and the fleet engineer was not impressed with you.'

'Oh, shit!' I thought.

Chapter 14

Life at Gulf

IN July I was given a week's holiday. Snuffy asked me if I was going away and I said, 'No, I can't afford it.'

He said, 'I have a chalet at Leysdown on the Isle of Sheppey and you can take the family there for a week.' I thought that was very kind of him, so Janne, my mother, the two girls and I had a nice week there. Snuffy came down for the weekend and stayed in another chalet that he owned so we got to see him too. It was our first real holiday together; Angela was two and a half and Lee-Anne was three months old.

After my father died, my mother said to us, 'Why don't you move in with me? You can have the upstairs flat and so when they demolish this house for slum clearance you will be re-housed.' So we left our flat and moved in with her and eventually the house was demolished to allow room for new housing.

My mother moved to a flat in Harlow, nearer to my sister, so I knew she would be all right. We, however, were offered a flat in Stratford which was not much better than my parents' old house, so we declined the offer and I told them that my work was moving to Grays so could I move out that way, and they offered us a flat in Aveley.

We had not lived in Aveley long when I wanted to sort something out at the bank. I parked the car in the pub car park, walked into the bank and asked the cashier if I could see the manager. She asked if I had an account with them and I said, 'Of course. Otherwise I wouldn't be here!' She got a diary out and said I could see him in two weeks' time.

'That's no good,' I replied. 'I want to see him sooner than that.' But I was basically told to take it or leave it. I threatened to withdraw my money and take it to another bank and she said that that was up to me.

However, it turned out that it was a good thing I didn't see him as I would have looked a complete fool.

I walked out from there rather wound-up at the thought that I had to wait two weeks to see the manager. I got in the car and looked at my bank on the other side of the road. As I sat there I thought, 'Where the hell have I been?' I had, in fact, been in the wrong bank.

So I got out of the car and walked into my bank and asked the cashier for an appointment with the manager. She said, 'We are closing in a short while, so I'll ask him if he will see you.'

The manager then came out and called me into his office. After a while he said they would have to close the bank while I was still having a consultation, then the phone rang and he excused himself to answer it. While he was on the phone he opened his cabinet and produced a bottle of Scotch with two glasses and beckoned to me to fill them. I looked behind me thinking he surely could not mean me. But no one else was there so I poured out two Scotches, and I sat there talking and drinking with the manager for quite a while.

What a difference between the two banks. Afterwards I told everybody what good terms I was on with the bank manager.

In the flat upstairs to us in Aveley there lived a Green

Line bus conductor with his son, who suffered with asthma. When the conductor asked me if I would take the boy out on a run any time, I said that of course I would. We were supplying all the American air bases, so I called round for him as I was going to Alconbury with the AEC Mandator artic.

When the opportunity arose on the way to the air base I put the pedal to the metal and was motoring. I kept my eye on the mirrors and there was no other traffic about so I gave it the gun. I was doing about sixty miles per hour and really motoring.

We were chatting away and every so often I looked in the mirrors. At first, there was no one behind, but when I looked again I nearly had a heart attack. A police car with lights flashing came from nowhere and was right on my back bumper. I started to slow down and indicated that I was looking for somewhere to pull up. The next thing I knew, he had overtaken me and waved a thank you at me for letting him by. I had thought my day had come.

On the way home I told the conductor's son that I was on a night out so I would park up at the Noak café and get a lift home. He said, 'Why don't you park in the garage at Aveley and walk home through the park and then in the morning walk back through the park to get the motor?' That sounded a good idea so I drove round to the garage and asked if I could park there and was told that I could.

The next morning I ran into the depot and filled in a night-out sheet which I booked off at Epping. However, we had a new depot manager who had come from the depot in Leith, Scotland, who said he was going to perform miracles with the way things were run, so the night shift had begun taking a new turn. He looked at my night-out sheet and said, 'You weren't in Epping last night, you were in Aveley, so go and alter your sheet. I'm not stopping your night-out money but you must put your sheet right.'

He then went on to say, 'Do you know where I'm lodging? I'm staying at Bulphan and I go home through Aveley – that is, until my wife and I find a house.'

Altering my sheet to Aveley only gave me half an hour run-in time as opposed to a one and a quarter hour run-in from Epping. I started to worry that I might be sacked, so I altered the sheet and when the shop steward found out he went mad and said I should have left it as it was; in his eyes I had cut the job up. But it was not his head on the chopping block. I saw the boy upstairs the next day and, laughing, I said, 'Don't give me any more advice!'

When we had two new six-wheel Albion Reivers with a splitter gearbox arrive home I volunteered to drive one. It was mostly on gas and diesel oil, or occasionally petrol. I used to do a lot of Bretts' sand and gravel pits in and around Kent and I once did a delivery to a pit on the Isle of Sheppey with two hundred gallons of diesel and two hundred of gas oil. I had been here often and never had any trouble so I was quite confident and started pumping into the diesel tank first, standing on top of the tank to dip it off. It was quite noisy, as the static tank was by the sea wall and on the other side of the road from me some cement mixers were being loaded.

Suddenly I heard a hissing sound, which was getting steadily louder. I looked all round to find out what it was and saw that someone had put a cap on the air vent of their tank. I kicked the foot valve down on the road tanker to stop any more diesel going into it and ran to get off the tanker, but I was too late. The tank blew up and diesel rained everywhere; I was soaked to the skin in it.

I walked into the office and the staff looked bewildered at the sight of me. I blurted out, 'Can you sign my delivery note please.' When it was signed I said, 'Oh yes, and by the way, can you order a new tank, yours has just blown up and the diesel is on the ground.' They rushed outside to find the tank split wide open.

'What bloody fool put a cap on the air vent?' I asked

'Oh, that was Charlie, he did not want the rain to get in.'

'Well, tell Charlie he won't need to worry about that now.'

The health and safety was called in and I had to say what had happened, but when they inspected the tank Charlie had removed the cap to cover his arse and I was blamed for pumping too fast. It did not matter how fast I pumped, it would not have blown the tank. I then had to drive back home smothered in diesel.

Another time I had a diesel delivery to a tipper firm in Rainham in Essex and while I was pumping off I stood talking to the yard foreman. Suddenly the hose burst and it was raining diesel everywhere. The foreman looked at me and said, 'Are you going to stop it?'

I looked at him and said, 'No, you can if you like, you have to run through the oil to stop it.' However, I knew it was my job, so I put my coat over my head and ran for it. I managed to shut it all down but once again I was drenched in diesel.

On another occasion I was delivering to Bretts' depot in Lydd, on Romney Marshes. They had a very small-gauge railway line with a few trucks. I connected to the tank on the other side of the railway and started to pump off the load. I then noticed two men talking by the side of the tank and before I could warn them not to stand near it while I was pumping, it came over the top. They both had to run, but it was too late again, they were drowned in gas oil.

Another time, I was out on the road with an AEC Mercury artic going up a slight incline when I went to change down a gear and the gear stick broke. I could not get any of the gears so I had to stop and find a phone box to report to the office. They said they would send a fitter out to me, who duly arrived and tilted the cab to remove the gear lever.

'I'll have to go and get a new one,' he said, so I had to wait with the tanker because I was loaded with petrol and it could not be left unattended.

While he went away I lay down on the grass verge and had a doze. After a few minutes I was woken by someone shaking me saying, 'Are you all right, driver?' I looked up to see a lady walking her dog. 'That must have been a shock for you when it tilted like that,' she continued. 'Are you badly shaken?'

I had to explain to her that I had broken down and that the cab had been tilted to get the part off. She looked at me with great embarrassment and said, 'Oh, I thought you were injured.'

'No, I am all right, but thank you for your concern.' So she carried on walking her dog.

Bretts were so unreliable when ordering their oil and Gulf were often to blame because they would send the loads a day early, not realising that the tanks were small and had no ullage room (space for extra oil). I always expected the unexpected when delivering to them. When we delivered to their earthmoving equipment we would be given a piece of paper with where to find them on it, which was always in some godforsaken place in Kent. You had to ride around for ages looking for them, I would even have to stop and climb on to the tank to survey the scenery. Once you'd found them you then had to wait while he drove over to you, with his little bowser tank for filling.

The Albion Reiver was slow and with the splitter gearbox you were changing gear all day and going nowhere. The other driver and I kept complaining about how sluggish they were until one Saturday I came into the terminal and was summoned to the office. I was told that on Monday morning I had to follow the fleet engineer to Haverhill in Suffolk to an engineering firm that worked with turbo AEC Mercury engines for coaches abroad and built racing cars. They were going to try and turbo the Albion.

The new depot manager decided to put more work on to the night shifts. This meant that the holiday period was over and so nobody wanted nights any more, but it was still a doddle. We used to deliver a lot to the western suburbs of London and on our way back we would stop at the Highway near Tower Bridge and as far as the eye could see there were tankers, of all companies, with the drivers in the pub supping up (I cannot imagine that happening now, the police would have a heyday).

This did not go down so well with my manager. We were in the local Working Men's Club in Purfleet once and he happened to be in there drinking and having some lunch. He saw the drivers come in, one by one, and didn't seem to mind, but when it was time to leave he nearly had a fit to see his whole transport fleet parked up outside. He went mental and we all kept out of his sight for a while. We were then told that no tankers were to be parked outside the club.

A year after I had taken the Albion to Haverhill to be updated they called to say that it was ready for collection. I had forgotten all about it by then, I never thought it would come back. We arrived at the firm, which was basically made up of sheds, and found that the motor had been out in the open fields for a year. I nearly cried when I saw it. I had to chuck the chickens out that were nesting in it; it looked a total disaster, but I cleaned the cab out as best I could and brought it home. A private haulier would not have suffered the amount of time that this vehicle was kept off the road.

On our first trip out the Albion started overheating, so it had to go back for the cooling system to be converted, but it was never the same and eventually they sent it to another depot. We were given two new six-wheel Leyland Bisons, which were much more powerful, but the noise was so atrocious that you needed ear muffs.

Again we complained and they sent my friend's one away for three months to be sound-proofed.

When it came back I couldn't stop laughing. All round the cab had been put cork matting or tiles; what a pig's ear they had made of it. I said I would rather put up with the noise than that. I had a couple of old car blankets which I put over the bonnet and made do with that.

A few weeks later, one of the drivers made arrangements for his wife to pick him up from the terminal. However, just as he was leaving, the dispatch clerk said, 'I have an urgent load of gas oil to go to Ladbroke Grove, west London and you are the only one available.'

The driver argued that his wife was waiting for him but they insisted he did it. Also waiting for him in the car was his little boy of about four years old, so he reluctantly went and took his boy with him for the ride.

He arrived at the delivery and got set up to off-load the gas oil while one of the employees stood on the top of their tank with his foot holding the delivery hose in the manhole (it was an open-top tank, always a disaster waiting to happen, and was not properly secured). The driver, in his haste to get back home, gave it some extra throttle so that with the force of gas oil going through it the hose stiffened and lifted up, throwing the employee off the tank.

The hose then came out of the tank and started swishing about in the air and finally made an entrance into the open nearside passenger door of the tanker cab, drowning the little boy in gas oil. There was a huge panic to shut it down. The office staff rushed the boy into the showers to clean him up and put something clean round him and keep him warm; he had been very frightened by his experience.

The cork insulation in the cab sucked up the gas oil like it was thirsty, so the motor could not be driven and had to be towed away for steam cleaning. A car was sent to pick up the driver and his little boy so the firm never knew that the boy had been in there.

When that motor came back you would get gas oil dripping on you as you drove along; it was never the same after. Ironically this was the only motor that had been sound-proofed.

If you asked any Gulf employee about my pet hate, they would say, 'taxi drivers.' We delivered to a lot of garages in London which served taxis, and one stands out in my mind. It was a small garage in Audley Street off Park Lane, west London, under a multi-storey car park. You pulled in between the kerb and the pump island, separated from the forecourt by a railing, which meant that you had to put the delivery hose across the pump island to the manholes on the other side.

Taxi drivers were always trying to beat you. I pulled in one day and stood talking to the guv'nor, when a cab came flying in and hit the wall on the other side of the pumps and smashed his nearside front wing in. I looked at him with contempt and said, 'Do you have to pass a special test to do that?'

He looked at me: 'Oh, funny bastard.'

'Well fancy coming in here at that speed.' I finished.

They tried to beat you by getting in before you closed the garage, so we tried to work with them. We would say, 'I'll back up as far as I can and you can fill up from the pump in front of me and when I'm finished let me move forward and then you can come and fill up behind me.' But they would always refuse to let you move and so we went back to shutting the site.

I pulled in one day and started getting the hoses off, when two taxis came flying in. I told them the garage was shut and they said, 'But you haven't started yet.'

'No,' I replied, 'because you're on the manholes.'

'Well, you can serve us and then unload.'

'If I let them serve you,' I said, 'then another taxi will come in and I'll have to let them serve him. The garage is shut, so if you insist on being served I'll take the load away.'

I then started to put the hoses back on the tanker, but the next thing I knew my head hit the side of the tank and I turned round to see that both the taxi drivers were going to attack me.

I started slogging it out with the one who pushed me; his face and shirt were black from my gloves which were covered in oil and dirt from the hoses. Just as I got one on the chin the boy cashier behind me started to use the phone (luckily they didn't have an office, only a hut on the pump island). The taxi drivers saw what the boy was doing and thought he was phoning the police, so they broke off from me, got in their cabs and flew out of the garage.

The boy said, 'The guv'nor wants to speak with you.'

I answered the phone and told him I was taking the load back, but he pleaded with me to drop the load and told me to get the boy to give me £10. So I agreed and dropped the diesel there.

When I got back I told the office and the shop steward so they called the garage and told them that we would phone when leaving the terminal and it would have to be shut when we arrived, without a taxi in sight, otherwise the delivery would come back. It became a bit of a joke at work because I was regarded as rather a quiet fellow. 'For God's sake don't upset Al,' they said. 'Otherwise he'll fight you.'

I had another run in with the taxi service when I was doing some part-time work on the coaches one weekend. I pulled out of the depot at Temple Mills, Leytonstone and drove across Hackney Marshes and noticed a taxi weaving in and out trying to pass me. I came to Mare Street and pulled up at the traffic lights to turn right into Richmond Road and he pulled up on my nearside and banged on the front entrance door (which had a glass panel). I looked across to him and he said, 'Can I come round you?'

That was fatal. I looked at him with contempt: 'No,' I said, pulling away. So he followed me all through Richmond Road.

I am not tarring all taxi drivers with the same brush; some must be quite normal. When the petrol industry had a strike the taxi drivers were all worried they would not be able to get any diesel. On the news they were griping that if they got below half a tank they would get airlocks. I never forgot this and would always tease them about it.

We eventually moved from our flat in Aveley to a house in South Ockendon. I once had a local delivery to Fords in South Ockendon when I had a sharp pain shoot through the left side of my rib cage after I had finished loading. As I had to pass so near home afterwards I thought I would call in for a cuppa. I pulled up to see Janne walking home from the papershop and I said to her, 'Do I look all right?'

'Why?' she asked, and I told her about the pain in my chest. Naturally she panicked and said she would phone the doctor.

I pleaded with her: 'I'll have a cuppa and some toast, and see how I feel.'

Still feeling no better, I said I would take the tanker back to the terminal and then see the doctor.

'I don't want you driving if you're not well,' she replied.

'It can't be helped. I don't want the firm to know.'

I went back to the terminal and told the traffic clerk I had been in the café for breakfast and did not feel well so I was going home. When I called into the doctor's on my way back he took my blood pressure and told me I was as fit as a fiddle, but should have a few days off.

When I pulled onto the drive at home, our next-door neighbour saw me and said, 'Hello, Al, you're home early!'

I told her about my pain. 'Don't take any notice of the doctor,' she said. 'Get up the hospital as they have a cardiac unit.'

So I told Janne where I was going and drove to the hospital. I walked into Accident and Emergency where the receptionist took my name and address and asked what nature of accident I had had. I said, 'I haven't had an accident, I have a pain in my chest.' She nearly fell off her chair then, and ran down the corridor.

The next thing I knew two nurses came running with a trolley which they got me on and pushed me to a room where they took my shirt off. Another nurse came in with the ECG equipment and wired me up. After a time I asked the nurse if anything showed up and she said, 'I'm not supposed to tell you, but to put your mind at rest: no.' Then she added, 'The doctor will come and see you now.'

The doctor came and told me that I hadn't had a heart attack and must have pulled a muscle. 'But I was just standing there,' I replied, 'filling up with diesel.'

'It could have happened earlier,' he said. So I had my few days off and then went back to work.

When I started back I was given a Guy Invincible with a four-in-line trailer tank. I had to do three deliveries around Luton, one being to Vauxhall Motors, and as the batteries on the truck were a bit naff I was told to call in at East Ham for replacements. I found the premises and saw that it was only a shop where they said, 'We only supply batteries, we don't fit them.'

I told the office this and asked if I should come back to have them fitted. I was hoping I wouldn't have to as it was getting late and I didn't want a night out, but I was told to carry on and do the deliveries.

The shop put the four batteries in the nearside of the cab and I carried on to Luton. As it was getting late I could only deliver to Vauxhall Motors and would have to do the other two in the morning. I drove back to Watling Street transport café at Markyate, but it was packed with trucks for the night and I could not lock the motor so I was worried someone would steal the batteries.

So I had something to eat and watched the television

until ten o'clock and went back to the truck and slept as best as I could across the engine cowling till the morning and then carried on with the deliveries.

On my way home I called indoors and realised that I looked like I had been dragged through a hedge backwards. I had a bath and something to eat and drove back to the terminal. That was the one and only time I had a night out in the thirty-odd years I was on the tankers. I learned a lot from the other drivers who parked up and left in the early morning; though that was back when we had log sheets and anything was possible.

In 1973 my mother died in Harlow Hospital at 75 years old. Again, it was a sad loss to our family and she will never be forgotten.

Chapter 15

The Last Stand

TIME was marching on and my daughters were getting older. When she was about ten years old Angela joined a baton twirling troop and two years later Lee-Anne joined. From there they joined an American-style marching band, as the colour guard. Angela was on rifles and Lee-Anne on flags; Lee-Anne stayed on until she was twenty-one.

One of the other fathers worked for a well-known second-hand bus dealer, who bought buses and sold them abroad. He coaxed his boss into letting the band lease two buses to take them about and so he gave them two Leyland Atlanteans, ex-BOAC (British Overseas Airways Corporation) buses that ran from Kensington to Heathrow. There was even a sealed-off area half-way through the downstairs saloon which had been a luggage compartment, which the band could use to store their uniforms. They also had a lorry for the instruments and a couple of helpers. I think there were about a hundred bandsmen and staff altogether.

I was approached by the band organiser and founder: 'I understand you hold a PSV licence, would you be available to drive one of the buses?' So I agreed. One of the other fathers, Reg, said that he used to drive buses and once held a PSV licence and he could drive the other bus, so Reg and I set about painting the buses in the band colours; they looked quite spectacular on the road. On weekends Janne and I would go with the girls on their gigs, we even went to Cornwall one time.

There was always lots of fund-raising going on. One of the fathers had a five-man bike, so the mothers said they would ride it from Southend to the half-way house on the A13, to London Main Road, to raise money.

When they finished, they said, 'Now it's the men's turn!' and one bright spark said, 'We will do John O'Groats to Land's End.'

Some of the fathers worked at Fords so they supplied a Transit minibus, one of them had a small camper van for cooking and Chambourcy supplied a load of yoghurts, which we had to pick up from Croydon.

We left on the Thursday morning. I was in the minibus with one of the drivers from Ford and another two drivers were in the camper. That left ten boys from the band to make up the two teams of five needed to man the bike; to say the least it was the most uncomfortable ride we ever had.

As soon as we arrived in the early morning at John O'Groats they got the bike out and started on their way, but after about a hundred yards the chain came off, which happened quite often. Also, the wheel on the front was a bit dodgy; basically it wouldn't work very well with five boys on it.

When we came to one hill the bike started gathering speed, but there were traffic lights at the bottom and a road coming in from the left with a garage on the apex. When the lights changed to red, they couldn't stop so they turned sharply left and went sailing through the garage until they came to a halt. Then they had to turn round to get back on route.

I had a go on the bike, but as we went through a town the kids started chasing us, taking the piss and pelting us with tomatoes. 'I've had enough of this,' I said, and got back in the van.

At one point we were coming down through a forest with the bike riders behind the van, my friend driving and me in the back watching the riders, when we came to a steep downward gradient. They started picking up speed again so I shouted to the driver, 'Go faster! They're catching us up!'

I'll never forget the look on those boys' faces as the brakes failed to slow them down, one boy was even shouting, 'We are all going to die!' They all had their feet on the ground to try and slow down and when they finally stopped, their trainers were worn through to their socks.

The only times we stopped were to fill up with petrol. The boys would then do a changeover; the ones on the bike would go in the camper and have some food while the second five took to the bike. The other driver and I took turns at driving and during the night the boys threw a tow rope out the nearside van window and we towed them along.

A couple of times I dropped off to sleep only to wake and find that the other driver was also dozing and we were going all over the road, so I made him stop and I took over. We eventually reached Land's End on the Sunday morning, but we had no time to celebrate as we were told that the mayor was going to welcome us home, so we drove back non-stop and arrived there at nine in the evening.

We had had hardly any sleep for about eighty-four hours so I was shattered. It was all a lark really; it was never recognised or recorded and we didn't make much money for the fund as, although we did do the John O'Groats to

Land's End, apparently we cheated by towing the bike at night.

In contrast to the colour and enthusiasm behind the events with the marching band, Purfleet's role in a local carnival was poor. The Gulf supervisor asked for volunteers to drive a vehicle that the company had entered. Nobody wanted to do it so I said I would drive it. The vehicle was an eight-wheel ERF and I said, 'Can I tart it up a bit and get it polished with some tyre black?' But I was told no, just take it as it is.

I took my sister's son with me and the people watching the procession were saying, 'Look at that poor sod, he's got caught up in the middle of the carnival,' not realising that we were part of it. I felt a right wally and didn't volunteer for anything after that, especially as the RAF had taught me not to put my hand up.

After the girls decided to leave the band there was no need for me to drive the buses and so they got a couple of the band boys to drive them, but they ran them with no water and so eventually they seized up.

Angela and Lee-Anne both left school at sixteen. Angela became a nurse and Lee-Anne went on to work for a Volvo distributor in Thurrock. We are proud of our daughters and their achievements.

Garry, our son-in-law, bought a new Ford XR3 and about a week later came round and said to me, 'Will you listen to my engine? It's popping and banging.'

I walked outside: 'You've filled it with diesel.'

'No I haven't,' he claimed. 'It had *petrol* on the pump.'

'You'd better go back to the garage,' I advised.

The attendant at the garage asked which pump Garry used. Garry pointed and the attendant said, 'Well it says *4 Star*,' and convinced Garry he had put petrol in.

When Garry told me this I took out a spark plug out and it reeked of diesel.

I said, 'It's definitely diesel.' So he went back and by this time there was a queue of cars popping and banging outside. The garage had to drain all the car tanks and then refill them with petrol. There were always thieves around who would take diesel to a garage and tell the guv'nor it was petrol and show him the dipsticks. Once it was in the underground tanks they had their money and it was down to the garage to sort it out.

We even had loads stolen out of the depot. A driver would load for an early start and come out to find it gone. Of course it had to be someone who would know it was loaded, so an inside informer was suspected. When I was at Bowen the Esso drivers once had a Union meeting in the office and a loaded tanker disappeared from right under their noses.

One Saturday, volunteers were called for to work on Sunday to take four loaded tankers to a distributor in the railway sidings at Banstead near Croydon and I was one of those who went. We arrived in convoy and each pumped off in turn. Three of us sat in one of the cabs larking about when I noticed the driver who was pumping off suddenly leg it as his hose burst.

I said to the other drivers, 'Look at that!' as the gas oil shot skywards. One of the drivers shot out of the cab and ran through the gas oil to shut it down. He called the original driver a few choice words as he had forgotten to open the delivery valve and of course he was now soaked in gas oil. 'What a brave man,' I thought.

Gulf was getting more garages and superstore contracts. I came off the six-wheel Bison and got a new Leyland Marathon artic. I must say I was not overly keen on the

Marathon as it stood quite high and had a box put on it for a cab; it looked like it had been a rush job to get it on the road and the stability just did not seem right.

I left Worthing and ran along the coast to Brighton and on my way back to Purfleet I decided to come over the South Downs. It was pouring with rain and as I started to climb up the hill I began losing traction and eventually stopped. 'This can't be right,' I thought, so I tried pulling away again but the wheels just spun.

I put on my wet-weather gear and left the motor to walk back down the hill, but half-way back I thought, 'Silly old me, I forgot I have a diff lock.' So I turned round and walked back up the hill to the motor. I got in and started it up and put the diff lock in and the wheels still just spun, so I had to get out again and walk all the way down the hill to phone the Gulf office.

They said they would get someone out to me, so I walked back up the hill again. I was not a happy bunny.

When we had really bad weather, such as snow, we used to keep the front compartment loaded so that there was weight on the unit drive axle. The trouble is there is not a lot of weight to move around when you are empty. A breakdown wrecker came to my aid and hooked a rope onto the front to tow me to the top of the Downs where he let me go. The driver said that he came out to these motors all the time on hills.

I had another accident in the rain due to this motor once when I was travelling from Tottenham and looking for the M25. It was pouring with rain and I was taking no chances so I crept along at a snail's pace; you could have walked faster, in fact I was holding traffic up, all because I had no faith in the motor. I approached the traffic lights at Bury Street and they were red so I stopped. From my right came a funeral hearse and the cortège, which proceeded to go in the same direction as me. The lights changed to green so I pulled away and followed the three cars in front of me and we all moved to the outer lane of the dual carriageway. Against my better judgment I started to overtake the funeral procession. The car in front of me was a Jaguar, in front of that was a Rover and then a Ford. I got alongside the funeral group and suddenly the Ford driver decided to turn right across the intersection onto the other carriageway.

I knew this was going to happen at some point, which was why I had been taking it slow. I tried the brakes and although I was not travelling fast they locked up and I hit the Jaguar, which in turn hit the Rover and then the Ford. I was more worried about the funeral procession, that maybe I would wipe them all out, so I looked for the trailer in case it had jackknifed, but it pulled up straight. While we sorted ourselves out the funeral went on its way. The Ford driver said she had realised she was going the wrong way and so had moved across the intersection.

To add insult to injury I heard a voice say, 'Hello, Uncle.' It was Janne's sister's son who was in the school opposite on his dinner hour. He said, 'Look, there's an accident over there and look, it's my uncle!' I was embarrassed to say the least.

I had another clash when I had to make a delivery to Tesco at Bar Hill near Cambridge once. I pulled onto the delivery point and after looking in the mirror I decided to get in a bit closer to it. The delivery points usually had a protection wall around them, nothing exciting and only one brick thick, but as I pulled in tighter and tried to get the gear lever out of reverse my foot slipped off the pedal, the motor leapt back and I saw the wall fall over.

I walked into the garage kiosk and the manager said, 'Cup of tea first, driver?'

'Yes please,' I said, 'and you'd better have a drop of Scotch in yours.' He started laughing and asked why. I said, 'I have just knocked your wall down.'

He still kept laughing: 'That's very funny. One of your drivers knocked that wall down six months ago and the bricklayer has just put it back up. Did you see the bricklayer leave or something?'

'No, I really have just knocked it down again.' He looked out the window this time and stopped laughing; he nearly cried. I said, 'While the cement is still wet I'll stack the bricks up again for you.'

'No you won't!' – As if I would.

I reported it to the depot manager when I got back. 'You're the third driver to knock it down,' he said. 'What's wrong with it?'

'It's in the bloody way, that's what's wrong with it.'

I was in the terminal one day and saw one of our tankers pull in; it had been on its maiden voyage after a repaint. I happened to notice that the nearside rear mudguard on the twin-trailer axle was missing and pointed this out to the driver who then informed the office. I was told to go with the driver and retrace his way back to the delivery to see if he could find it. I thought that surely someone would notice a mudguard and so we kept stopping and asking people. Eventually a man said, 'Yes, it's in the fire station.' So we made our way to the fire station to be told, 'It's at the police station now.'

So we went to the police station and enquired if they had a mudguard from a lorry. The station sergeant said, 'Can you give me a description of it?'

I thought, 'How many mudguards fall off lorries around here? He must be some kind of nut.'

We said, 'Well, it's black and it goes over the top of two-axle wheels.' He then got a big ledger book out and said it was in the car park. We walked out to the car park and saw that it was taking up a car space, so we got one end each and walked to the tanker; it looked like we were carrying a coffin. We pushed it back onto its runners and returned to the depot for the fitters to refit it.

I had a much more serious run-in with the police on another occasion. I was on nights and had a delivery in London. On my way home it was pouring with rain and I was travelling along Commercial Road behind three cars, with nothing behind me. When we approached Cotton Street traffic lights, a T-junction coming from the right, being high up above the cars, I could see that the car in front of us was going to turn right.

I knew there was nothing behind me, but I still looked in the mirror to make doubly sure. I then indicated and pulled to the nearside lane. There was an almighty crash!

I couldn't think what it could have been and my immediate thought was that it was a motorcyclist. I stopped and got out the cab and walked to the nearside and could not believe my eyes. A car had mounted the kerb, gone through the railings and the front was embedded in a Chinese restaurant.

They were trying to get the driver out from the nearside door and panic reigned in the restaurant; they thought they were under attack.

The driver of the car asked whether I was the tanker driver.

When I confirmed I was, he asked, 'Can you wait here

until the police come?' I thought he was joking – how could I possibly leave all this?

A man came to the driver and reassured him that his wife and child were all right. 'They're in the fish shop,' he said.

I hadn't seen anybody else get out of the car. The police then arrived and one of them interviewed me, while the other one interviewed the driver. The policeman asked if we could sit in the cab as it was pouring with rain. I explained what had happened and said that I didn't know where this car had come from.

'The driver of the car said he was stationary,' the policeman told me.

'No way,' I said.

There was no damage to the tanker so I could only assume that he hit one of the super-single trailer tyres and bounced off it. After getting back to the terminal, I made out an accident report and went to see the manager. I explained that I still did not know where this car had come from and that I thought maybe he had come out of a road on the left.

The manager told me to take his car and ride up and have a look. I was right, there was a road on the left.

I had the option of a company or union lawyer and I chose the company one. I had to go to the crown offices at the Temple, London and in no uncertain terms they told them I was at fault for changing lanes.

I heard no more for some time. A few months passed, until a time when we returned home from Cornwall with our caravan. After unpacking I went for a bath and at about 10.30 pm the phone rang and Janne called me to come and speak to a policeman. He said, 'We've been trying to reach you, where have you been?'

I told him that I had been on holiday.

'You have to be in court on Monday,' he said, 'but it has been adjourned, so don't come. You won't come, will you?'

I agreed: 'If you say don't come then I won't.'

Then he stressed again that I was not to appear in court. This was all news to me; I hadn't heard a thing.

He ended by saying, 'We will let you know when the next hearing is. You won't come, will you?' I thought this was all a bit strange.

A few weeks later I had a letter telling me to appear at Arbour Square Police Courts in the afternoon. So I sat waiting there with a load of prostitutes, drug addicts and thieves and saw from the notice board that I was the first case at 2.30 pm.

The usher called out a man's name which meant nothing to me and then a lawyer came through the door making a bee-line for me.

'Mr Heymer?' he asked.

I nodded and he said, 'I am your brief and I am going into the court to see what is happening.'

When he came back out, he continued, 'The prosecuting sergeant wants you to plead guilty.'

'No way,' I replied.

'I have already told him that,' he said, going back into court.

When the lawyer reappeared, he asked, 'How many times have they postponed the hearing?'

'Only once, when the officer phoned me.'

'No,' he said, 'it's been three times.'

'Well I didn't know anything about it.'

By this time I was on my own in the court waiting-room as everybody had been in and gone, so the police had no option but to have me in because I was there.

The lawyer then came out again and said, 'This is your lucky day, because for some reason the car owner will not come to court, and that's why they have been cancelling the hearing. I think maybe he is an illegal immigrant, so all you have to do is say, "not guilty".'

When I entered the court the sergeant looked at me and was asked by the judges to read the charges. He listed: dangerous driving and driving without due care and attention. I was then asked how I pleaded. 'Not guilty,' I said.

The sergeant then addressed the bench. 'I am sorry, Your Honour, but the prosecution witness refuses to come to court, so we have no charges to offer.'

The judges looked at me with a faint smile: 'Mr Heymer, you are free to go.'

I came out of the court and the lawyer shook my hand saying, 'It was nice meeting you.'

Outside the court, the police sergeant asked, 'Are you the tanker driver?'

I confirmed I was.

'What did you get?'

When I told him that I was let off, he suddenly went off on one and started shouting: 'We were going to nail your arse to the wall!'

'I'd like to see you try, you bastard!'

The car was a write-off and the Chinese restaurant was very damaged. I still don't know what really happened.

I returned to the depot one morning from a delivery and was asked if I would take a motor already loaded to a garage, as they were nearly out of petrol. I went through the vehicle checks but did not check the load as I had the loading meter tickets. On my way out of the depot I passed one of the drivers who was starting on the midday shift and I waved to him but he looked worried and I thought 'What's wrong with him?'

When I arrived at the garage the manager checked the load and said, 'You have some extra on board.'

I told him that I didn't know as the motor was already loaded when I got it.

'How much do I owe you, then?' he asked.

'I don't know.'

'Will you be satisfied with £50?'

'You want to give me £50?' I said, and he nodded. 'Bloody hell,' I thought, 'how much extra was there?'

When I arrived back at the depot I found three of the drivers waiting for me, demanding the money. They told me that the load had been set up for the driver I had passed coming to work, so no wonder he looked grim. But I argued that had I got caught on the road, would they have owned up and got me off the hook? I didn't think so, so I would keep the £50.

Then the driver who set the load up said he wanted his share and was not worried about the other two, so I gave him £25 and said to myself that in future I would check the load and if it was wrong I wouldn't move the vehicle.

I found out later that they told the traffic clerk to make sure the late-starting driver did the load but the clerk said that because the garage had nearly run out it had to go as soon as possible.

I had a further close call with some extra in the load on a delivery to another garage. Snuffy said to me, 'You know what to do and where to take it?' and I said I did. I was delivering to the garage and standing on top of the tank waiting for a dry dip when the manager said, 'You're wanted on the phone.'

So I jumped down and it was one of the drivers asking if I would change shifts with him. I then came back to try the dips and it had gone down, or so I thought, so I changed compartments and started the same procedure.

Just as I was getting a dry dip the manager said, 'You're wanted on the phone again.' So I jumped down and it was the office asking if the driver had been in touch with me. I got back on the tank and thought that it must have been done by now.

I arrived at the place that bought extras and said, 'I don't think there is much in there but have a try.'

He rolled out a forty gallon drum and I thought, 'He has some hope.' However, he filled it and went away for another drum and filled that and said to me, 'I thought you said there wasn't a lot in there?'

'Well, that's what I thought.'

I saw Snuffy the next day and told him what had happened. 'Oh,' he said, 'I forgot to tell you I sawed an inch off the sticks.'

'Blimey,' I thought, 'it's a good job I had the phone calls otherwise I would have come away with half the load.' Of course, the practice of making our own dipsticks if they broke stopped and now the sticks have to be custom stamped.

When we had our yearly party for the staff, all the other depots were invited too. As I was standing talking to some mates the depot manager came up to me and said to another man at his side, 'This is the man you want.'

I looked surprised and the man said, 'I am the depot manager from Cardiff. We have your old Leyland Marathon and the driver allocated it could not believe his luck with how clean and polished the motor had been kept.'

'Are you taking the Mickey out of me?'

'No, when a vehicle comes from another depot they always give you the shit ones, not the best.'

'Well, in that case, thank you very much,' I said.

I was known as a bit of a bullshitter for keeping my vehicle clean and polished, so much so that the drivers were afraid to take it out and get it dirty, especially on nights. When I was on nights I always wondered what state I would get it back in when I went back to days. I thought it made sense to keep it clean. I spent more time in the cab then at home, so why sit in a pigsty?

In 1982 I was called to the office to see the manager. 'How would you like to take early retirement?' he asked.

I looked behind me to see if he was talking to someone else: 'I am only fifty years old.'

'I know, but there's an opportunity if you want it.'

'I'll sleep on it,' I said, 'and let you know.'

Two weeks later I parked up at the Noak café on a night out and a couple of our drivers were there talking. One said, 'You missed all the action this morning, the custom officers shut the terminal and arrested five of our drivers for fiddling petrol; you got out just in time.'

The guv'nor then had me back in and said, 'Under the circumstances I can't let you go until we know the outcome of the court case; as soon as they are found guilty they are sacked.' Apparently they had been operating on a big scale, even including local businessmen, and had been filmed from the telephone exchange. After a year of waiting for the court hearing they were all found guilty and sacked, so I was saved.

I used to load out of a Total depot in Slough to take to Tesco in Newbury, Wiltshire. On arriving one time I went in for a cuppa before I started unloading. After a while the manageress and I went out to the tanker and something attracted me to the sight glass on the tank outlet pipes; I saw that they were full of water. I said, 'I'm sorry, but I will have to take this load away as it has water in the petrol.' I phoned the depot and was told to take it back to Slough.

When I arrived back at the terminal the supervisor asked, 'What's all this about water in the petrol? You've got some cheek, saying we have water in our fuel.' He proceeded to water-dip it with the paste and then declared, 'You're right, pull over the drain and open your valves,' and water flowed out.

As soon as the petrol started coming out I shut the valve (the drains in the terminal go into a tank that separates the water) and then went to have the petrol sucked off by special pump.

In the late 1980s, contractors were coming onto the scene and telling the oil companies how much they could save them on their transport. We were told by the shop steward that under no circumstances would we be taken over by contractors, but in 1988 our shop steward went on holiday and just as he got on the plane we received a letter saying that we would be taken over by Tankfreight, a subsidiary of the NFC (National Freight Company) and we would have to apply for a job. Funnily enough the shop steward was given a job in their office at Harrogate.

I filled an application form in and wondered if, at fifty-six, I stood a chance. There were twenty-seven drivers at Gulf and most of them did one load a day and carried their golf gear in the cab. Tankfreight said they could do the same work with seventeen drivers, and they were probably right. They said they would get rid of the mixed transport fleet and use only 38-tonners; we thought they were mad, how can you get a 38-tonner in a garage that could hardly get a four-wheeler in? But we were told: 'You are a Tankfreight driver now and you can do the impossible.'

We had to have the interview at a local hotel. One by one we went in and when it came to my turn there were three men from Tankfreight sitting there and the first thing they said to me was, 'Don't worry about your age.'

I said thank you and they proceeded to ask me questions, such as what did I think of contractors coming onto the scene?

I replied that it was not up to me what the company decided, and then one of them said to me, 'I see you drove touring coaches for Galleon.'

I said, 'Yes, that's right,' and thought 'what have coaches got to do with tankers?'

He then went on to tell me that he had been the transport manager for a well-known coach company up north in his earlier working life and had I heard of them, to which I said yes, I had.

The interview was then over and we shook hands. I don't know why but I suddenly said, 'Good luck in your new venture.'

'Thank you very much,' they replied. I later wondered why I came out with that, but it had just rolled out of my mouth.

Some of the drivers went in with guns blazing and told them where to stick their job and that they would not work for them at any cost. I thought, 'Well, why go for the interview, then?' Anyway they already knew who they wanted; they would get rid of the dead wood.

When drivers had been with Gulf for ten years they got a gold tie-pin with a small diamond in it (it was small, but the thought was there), inscribed with the Gulf name and the number of years served. After fifteen years you got a gold tie-pin with a diamond and a ruby, and after twenty years it came with a diamond, ruby and sapphire. I received my ten-year and fifteen-year, but I ended up two days short of my twenty years. Gulf said they wouldn't give me the award, even when I asked for it. However, I did receive a fifteen-year tie pin from Chevron, which was part of the company. I found this very strange.

Shortly after my interview I received a letter stating that I had a job, what the wages were and that I would start on a certain date with the other selected drivers. I arrived on the Monday morning and was given my ERF and tandem-axle trailer. I did the same work as before, only faster and for less money, but at least I had a job. In time we were issued with a new uniform and shirts and ties which we were told to wear, especially the ties, as they made us look professional.

I was on nights once when two of us had a bridging delivery to Oakley in Bedford, a small independent oil distributor. While we were pumping off into their storage tanks we looked around to see what was on offer. I found a scaffold board which I threw on top of the tank and my mate found some electric light tubes which he put in the cab. Then we left the depot.

At the time we did not have automatic reversing lights, we only had a switch in the cab, and my mate had a bad habit of using them if a lorry flashed him in. I was going to tell him how dangerous it was, but I did not like criticising another driver, so I let it ride. However, I should have, as when we were coming back down the motorway and he was in front I saw a police car coming down the slip road, so my mate moved out to the centre lane and the police car flashed him in and he gave them the two reversing lights. They were like spot lights and lit the road up so much that they chased him and stopped him and I carried on past.

I wondered if someone had seen us take the things from the depot, or whether they were telling him off about the lights. When we got back to the terminal I asked what they stopped him for and he said they told him to put his reversing lights on and then get out the cab and walk round the back of the tank. 'How would you like someone flashing them lights at you in the dark?' they said. You completely blinded us, so don't use them like that again.'

We eventually got to the depot and as we entered the gatehouse the security guard said, 'Watch out for the old boy wandering around the terminal.' I thought that maybe he had come off a ship docked there and so we parked the motors and looked around; it was pitch dark but we saw him crouched under the loading racks. When we saw his face we both wanted to run as he was an ugly git with long silver hair down to his shoulders.

I don't know which of the two of us was more frightened, but my mate soon made his excuses and shot off home. I told the gatekeeper I was going to take the van and my scaffold board home which would only take me half an hour and then I would come back. When I returned I parked the van and, looking over my shoulder for the old man, half ran up to the gatehouse. The security guard said, 'Come in for a cuppa before you leave.'

'Where's the old boy?' I asked.

'He's in here with me, having a cuppa. Come and see him, he's harmless enough.' So I walked in, sat down and kept looking at the old man. He looked a right old tramp and in the half-lit hut you really couldn't make him out, but then I noticed his shoes which were highly polished and I began to twig that he was one of the security guards who would go round in the van calling in to make sure the terminal security guards were OK.

He then took the mask off. We had a good laugh and I told them my mate was shitting himself (forgetting to say I was as well). He went on to say that he put the mask on in the morning when the staff were arriving and threw stones at them so that they would think he was a right weirdo.

I had another funny encounter when I was doing a delivery to a garage in Bognor. While I was unloading, a group of ducks ambled round me and then started wandering in the road. I held all the traffic up while they walked across and then something frightened them and they flew off, leaving me in the middle of the road. I ran into the garage and said, 'All your ducks have flown off.'

'They aren't mine,' he said. 'They're wild and come here for something to eat.' I felt a right wally.

When I was on nights once, as I came to the Rainham traffic lights, I was pulled in by custom officers, one of whom said, 'We want a sample from your running tank.'

'What for?'

'We're checking for red diesel.'

'You must be kidding me. This is an oil company.'

'We don't trust anybody,' he said and proceeded to take out diesel which they checked in their van. They came out eventually and said I could go.

We delivered to a garage in south London which had an Alsatian dog. When we got the manholes up he would run off with the fittings and you had to chase him round the garage to get them back. He thought it was great fun. I don't know how he could pick them up because they were so heavy, but it did break up the monotony.

Another time, while at Gulf, I was stopped by the weights and measures inspectors, just before running into Canterbury. I was taken to the weighbridge and told that I was over-weight on the front axle and to inform the company. Some time later I was pulled in again at the same place and was put in a queue of traffic waiting to go on the weighbridge.

One of the inspectors came walking along, stopped at me and asked, 'What are you doing here?'

'I was told to come to the weighbridge.'

'Bloody fools! How can you be overweight? You can only put in what your tank will hold. Off you go.'

'He knows a lot,' I thought.

I had a delivery in the West End of London and turned off the Embankment into Northumberland Avenue, approaching Trafalgar Square and sat in the nearside lane of the traffic hold-up. Just then a three-ton Ford box van came down the outside lane and swiped my mirror, knocking it round; the driver made no attempt to apologise and stopped just forward of me, but as the traffic moved I got alongside him and banged on his nearside door window and we ended up shouting at each other.

The traffic then started moving and as I was the slower of the two of us he shot across in front of me and was looking at me in his mirror throwing scorn at me. I could see the funny side of this and started laughing.

But when he saw me do this he stopped, put his vehicle into reverse and came flying backwards into the front of my vehicle. I managed to get my legs up out of the way just as the motors collided, causing glass to crash around everywhere as the headlights smashed. He sped away, but I managed to get his number plate.

I pulled round the corner and saw a policeman standing

there. I reported it to him and he said he would get the traffic police here.

When the squad car arrived they said that we would have to go to Cannon Row police station.

I explained that where he reversed into me there was a pedestrian refuge and anybody crossing between the vehicles would have been crushed.

The officer rode in the tanker with me, directing me down Pall Mall and into St James's Park. 'I'm not allowed through here,' I said but he replied that it was all right and parked me up in Whitehall. He wrote a note saying I was in Cannon Row police station and left it on the windscreen.

I gave a statement about what had happened. They informed me that he wouldn't get far.

After some time they told me that I must have got the plate wrong as, according to Swansea DVLA, that number was for a Ford Cortina.

'Could it have had false plates,' I suggested. 'If I had false plates I could go round doing things like that.'

They said 'no', but I thought 'yes', because I knew I did have the right number.

On occasions we were sent on day courses involving fire fighting, driving and health and safety in the work place. We were taken out into the terminal where they had a road tanker filled with water. The instructor would open the valves so that the water would rush out and we had to remove the hoses. We were shown how to use them to encircle the water and were given some form of paper-mâché to tuck under the hose to stop seepage from entering the drains. This paper-mâché was then carried on the tankers as one of the safety measures.

We then had to learn some fire fighting. They had a large water trough with some petrol on top of the water set alight and we were expected to get the right extinguisher for that type of fire and put it out. We also did driving courses where we had to drive forwards and reverse round obstacles in both rigids and artics.

As part of our health and safety at work courses the company nurse came to show us First Aid including how to put patients in the recovery position and give them the kiss of life. She lay down on the floor and the manager showed us mouth-to-mouth resuscitation and we couldn't wait for our turn. But then they brought the dolls in; it was such a let-down. All these courses took a day each and after these we had some written tests.

This was all part of safety on the road, but then you still had to contend with the public. I once pulled onto the delivery point at a garage and was walking towards the kiosk when I passed a young lady who was smoking while she was filling her car.

I looked at her and said, 'Don't tell me that cigarette is alight.'

In response, she pushed her hand with the cigarette behind her back to hide it. I told the garage manager who gave her a right telling off. This was only one of the stupid things you came up against.

On these courses we were shown films of forecourt fires and tankers blowing up; if you thought about it too much you wouldn't be able to do the job. Sometimes people would ask if I worried about fire and I would say, 'Well, until someone mentions it to you it's out of your mind. But you always treat the load with the respect it deserves.'

*   *   *

In March 1997 I was having severe back trouble, so I was
off sick for a long time, until Tankfreight sent me to see a
company doctor in October.

'Why have you waited this long?' he said. 'You retire in
December, don't you?'

When I confirmed it, he told me to rest at home on
sick-leave until then.

I was sixty-five years old. I had been working non-stop
for fifty-one years, forty-seven of which had been full
of driving. I had been at Gulf for twenty years and
Tankfreight for nine, so the drivers bought me a watch as a
leaving present.

I have always felt that from the day I was born my life had
already been planned out. I wanted to follow in my father's
footsteps and be on the road and, although I could have
pursued this in a number of different ways, working on
long-distance or continental trips and so on, my life's map
seemed to be set out for me.

Not that I have any regrets. I never had any ambitions to
further myself through promotion as I was happy in the
work I did. A few of the younger drivers finished up as
clerks and transport managers, but I didn't want to be stuck
in an office. The pay in the oil trade was higher than in
general haulage, so I earned a good wage to support my
family.

I have driven HGV vehicles up to 38 tons including
rigids and articulators. I've had to master all kinds of gearboxes: autos, semi-autos, pre-selectors, crash boxes, gate
change, range change and splitters. My public service
vehicles have been electric-powered trolley-buses, petrol
and diesel single and double-decker coaches and buses.

I've sailed close to the wind at times, but during my

forty-seven years on the road I've got through with no
convictions.

Now I can sit back and look back over the events of
the past few years, and know that I did what I was meant
to do.

Chapter 16

Part-Time

WHEN I stopped doing seasonal work on the tours and started full-time employment on the tankers, I couldn't wait for the summer to come around so I could help out on the coaches. I used to go to the garage to see if I could do some part-time driving at weekends like my father did; I have a few stories to tell about that.

One weekend I was given a Sunday afternoon job to pick up a load of children who had been camping with their school at Horsham in West Sussex and take them home to Gants Hill and Chigwell. Eventually I found the camp and saw that there were a couple of other coaches waiting too. A teacher approached me and asked, 'How do you want to load the children's gear?'

'Is there any way in particular you want it done?' I asked. He said not.

'In that case, I'll load the Chigwell first and then the Gants Hill. Then I can go straight back to Leyton.' This is what we agreed.

I sat back in the coach and opened the front entrance door. Then on to the scene came two lady teachers who started shouting, loud enough for me to hear: 'It comes to something when the driver starts dictating which way we have to go!'

I got out of the coach. 'Is there a problem, ladies?' I asked.

The stouter of the two replied, 'Yes, I want you to go to Gants Hill first. I have made arrangements with the mothers there to pick up their children at eight o'clock, bearing in mind that we are leaving at four o'clock.'

'Why have you said eight o'clock?' I queried. 'I'll have you home by a quarter past five.'

She looked at me: 'Don't be so ridiculous, Driver. It took the other man four hours to get us here and you're telling me you'll do it in one and a quarter hours? I hope you're not going to speed with children on board.'

I asked which way the other driver had come and she replied that it was through London. 'Well, I'm going home on the motorway,' I said. I knew it would only take an hour and a quarter because I did it with a tanker all the time. I thought, 'I'll get you there in that time, no matter what the cost.'

We left at four o'clock and I had a good run up the M23, on to the M25 and through the Dartford Tunnel. We pulled up at Gants Hill at quarter past five, in torrential rain. The teacher looked at me and said, 'I suppose you think you're clever now. What am I going to do with these children in the rain? I'll have to phone all the parents to come and collect them.'

I said, 'I'm sorry, but what do you want me to do, ride round for three and a quarter hours? If you had let me do Chigwell first you would have had another three-quarters of an hour on the coach.' I unloaded and felt sorry for the children, but it was not my fault that the other driver took four hours.

When I got back to the garage I told the manager that he may receive a complaint about me and explained what had taken place. He said, 'How did it take him four hours?'

'You tell me,' I answered.

One Friday afternoon when I finished work I had a phone call from the Galleon manager asking if I would be able to take a coach up to Edinburgh overnight, as one of the vehicles on tour had somehow broken a window and they needed a relief coach. I said I would do it.

I popped across the road to my friend Ron who had been a lorry driver, but now worked in the docks and asked him if he'd like to come for a ride.

We drove from South Ockendon to Leyton in the car and picked up the coach which had been fed and watered and carried on our way. We took turns at the wheel and when we arrived at about eight o'clock in Edinburgh drove round to the hotel to find the driver. He took us to the coach that we had to bring back and then we went back to the hotel for some breakfast and drove home. Back in London there was a bread strike, so on our way back we stocked up with bread and brought it home for the neighbours.

When I was touring there were not a lot of motorways, so it took two days to get to Edinburgh, but now they do it in one day. Some weekends we would do a changeover. A driver would take the coach to Kings Cross, load it and then take it to Keele or Knutsford services. The tour driver would be with you on the back seat and he would then take over and drive the rest of the way up to Edinburgh. We would then cross the motorway to the other side and wait for the one coming down and drive him home.

I did this one weekend and was waiting for my ride home when I saw my coach coming down the motorway.

I walked out to the car park, only to see the back end of the coach as he disappeared out of the service area. I could not believe it. I phoned the garage and told the manager that he hadn't even stopped and he said, 'Get on a rattler and come home.'

I had very little money on me so I vowed I would never be caught out like this again. I started trying to thumb a lift, very thankful that it was a lovely summer day, although I was sweating. I didn't seem to be having much luck with this, so I decided to walk into Knutsford. I threw my coat over my shoulder and came into the town. I found the station and asked how much it was to London, but I didn't have enough for the fare and my plight fell on deaf ears. The station staff said it would have been better to stay at the services and get a lift.

So I started walking back to the services and saw a coach pass me which pulled into a nursery for its passengers to buy some flowers. I went into the nursery, found the driver and explained my predicament, and he very kindly dropped me off at the services. I stood for ages looking for a lift and then a car pulled up and said he was going to Coventry. I was thankful for small mercies after this, as I had just enough for my rail fare home from Coventry station.

I got to Stratford station and started walking back to Leyton. On the way I passed a pub and thought, 'I'm gasping, I'll have a pint.' The door was open and I said to the girl, 'Can I have a pint of bitter, please?'

She looked at me and said, 'You'll be lucky, we shut half an hour ago. It's eleven o'clock.'

'Well, that figures,' I said and walked back to the garage to get my car. There were only the cleaners and the fitters getting the coaches ready for the next day. On the notice board there was a note asking me to take the driver who left me at Knutsford back to Knutsford in the morning. I got out a pencil and paper and wrote: 'You drove yourself home, now drive yourself, back,' and walked out.

The driver in question had in fact been a very good friend to me when I had been touring, so he was full of apologies. He said he had a good laugh at my note when we met up again and said, 'There are a lot of drivers I would be willing to leave behind, but not you Al.'

It turned out that he had been used to having a regular driver who always stood in one place in the car park, so when he saw nobody standing there he drove out rather than stopping and wasting time.

He often said to me, 'Park your car down the road and I'll take it to Edinburgh and you can go home,' but I always worried in case something went wrong.

I was asked to do another changeover at the end of the summer season, so arrangements were made for me to get a lift on a coach to Keele services to wait for the coach coming home from Edinburgh.

I met the driver going away on tour and we went to Kings Cross to load. When I made myself scarce and sat on the back seat, a young girl came and sat down beside me. After we had been going a while we reached our first stop at the services for coffee, so I sat down with the driver and then this girl came and sat with us again. I thought this was rather strange, but he introduced me and she turned out to be his bit on the side.

He said to me, 'When we leave here you can drive the coach and I will sit at the back with her.'

I replied, 'I'm not getting paid to drive you, only to drive the one coming home.' We argued the fact and as we came out of the restaurant he went to the toilet and I thought, 'This is my opportunity to get back on the rear seat.'

He boarded the coach and shouted to me, 'Are you going to drive, then?' All the passengers looked round to see who he was speaking to and this carried on for a bit, him shouting out asking if I was going to drive and the passengers having no idea who I was.

In the end I said, 'All right, but you'll have to show me how to start it and how the gears go.'

He said, 'Well, come up the front and I'll show you.' I got behind the wheel and he showed me how to start the coach and how the gears went, and said, 'Will you be all right, then?' I said I would give it my best shot.

I turned round to the couple sitting in the front and said, 'This is the first tour I've been on where the passengers do some of the driving.'

The man said, 'I'm game if you are.'

'Nice one,' I thought.

I kidded around with the passengers again on another occasion. I once arranged a weekend trip to Blackpool with neighbours and staff from a local Tesco store, but the manager at Galleon said, 'I can't let you drive it because I have drivers standing about.' So we loaded up and got to Keele services on the M6 and I went and sat with the driver. I asked him what his plan was and he said, 'Well, I'll drive you to Blackpool and we will go through the lights, then I will drop you at the hotel and get a rattler home.' The coach was staying with us and a relief driver was coming up to take us home.

'Where do you live?' I asked.

'Newcastle.'

'Well, if you like, I'll take the coach up to Blackpool and you can go home from there.'

He didn't want telling twice: 'That's lovely, I'll be able to take the old woman out for a drink; she will be pleased.' We all got back on the coach. The driver said goodbye and have a nice weekend, picked up his briefcase and walked away. The passengers had no idea about what we had decided, so they looked at me and said, 'Where's he going?'

I said, 'His hours are up and so he's going home.'

They looked at me sitting in the coach: 'So what happens to us?'

'Well, I could have a go if you like.' I sat in the driver's seat, making out that I was looking for something. I started the coach and slipped it into reverse gear and let the clutch out a bit quick and the coach took a leap back and some of the women tried to make a dash for the exit. Janne had to explain that I was sodding about and got them to return to their seats. I took them on to Blackpool.

Not everyone got my humour. One weekend I was given a party of Americans to take to Stratford-upon-Avon and London. One lady said, 'On the Continent we swap seats each day; do you do it here?'

I said, 'No, Ma'am, the only time you will change seats is when I change gear.' She looked at me a bit strangely then.

I had a great laugh one time when I was one of six coaches taking some East End children to Southend for the day. We all got there quite early so one of the drivers said, 'I'm going for a haircut.' So we all decided to have one.

We found a barber shop, but he was not open yet and when eventually he came round the corner he was quite surprised to find he had a queue waiting at that time in the morning. He thought things were looking up in the trade. We all had a haircut and a shampoo.

One driver had hardly any hair at all, so the barber asked him if he wanted a shampoo and I said, 'No, just wipe the flannel over his head.' He was, incidentally, the driver from Aero who kept blowing the hoses.

I remember one strange occurrence when I was doing a day's work with a well-known second-hand bus distributor, who bought buses from the home market and then sold them abroad; he operated the London tours with open-top, ex-London Transport DMS buses. During the day I had to stop in a traffic jam in the city and a young girl of about eighteen jumped out of the car in front of me and gave me a big red rose. It made my day; all the traffic seemed to disappear after that.

I used to deliver petrol to a big Tesco store where the young manager in the garage always asked me about my time on the coaches until one day he said, 'I think I will go for lessons and get a PSV.'

He eventually passed but then he said, 'I can't get work because I have no experience.' A friend of mine had four coaches so I approached him to see if he could help the young manager and he said, 'Tell him to come and see me.'

I relayed the message and my friend gave the lad some school runs to do and sometimes a theatre trip. He would get in his car and drive up to the theatre to find his way and then in the evening take the party of people in the coach. This friend of mine had big ideas and wanted to do more continental work, so he said to the Tesco lad, 'Give me a £1,000 and you can have the old coach and the school contract,' which he did.

I said to him, 'In the evenings, go round the social clubs and make yourself known, then you can start taking the old folk down the coast.' He did this, too, and while my friend went broke trying to get continental work, the Tesco lad has now got four Volvo B10s. He says I was his mentor and that it was me who got him where he is today.

One weekend my manager said, 'I haven't got any work for you, but an owner-driver has gone sick so I was wondering if you would do his job for the day?'

He told me that in Walthamstow car park there was a Bedford six-wheel VAL coach, a twin steerer, so I made my way to the car park and found the coach and the hidden key, checked the oil and water and started it up. I moved across the car park and applied the brakes as I came up to the main road, but there were no brakes. I grabbed the handbrake and the Bedford eventually stopped, so I reversed it back to where I had got it from and locked it up.

I then went back to Galleon and told him what had happened and that he would have to phone the tour company and tell them that their London tour wasn't running. 'Please don't find me work like that again,' I said.

I was put on hire to Grey-Green coaches out at Mile End garage (Galleon later moved to these premises) and told to follow a coach going to Dovercourt and Harwich to pick up the over-load. When we stopped for a tea break the Grey-Green driver said to me, 'When we get to the Dovercourt holiday camp, I'll take the Harwich passengers and you can pick up a full load and take them back to the East End and drop them off.'

When we arrived at Dovercourt the staff said, 'Go and get a tea, driver, and we'll load the coach for you.' When I returned they told me I was ready to go, so I jetted back to the East End, dropping off all round Bethnal Green and

Aldgate and the passengers said, 'Blimey, you took half the time that the driver took!'

I replied, 'Well, I don't hang about,' and on my way past Mile End I dropped my return tickets into their office. I then arrived back at the Galleon garage at about six o'clock and the manager called me into the office. 'Where have you been?' he asked. I told him what had happened and he said, 'Grey-Green want to know where their five o'clock service coach from Harwich is and why it is that you haven't worked for them today.'

I said, 'I have! How did the passengers from Dovercourt holiday camp get home if I was not there?'

He said, 'Where are your tickets?'

'I handed them in at Mile End,' I replied.

So he said, 'Well get in your car and go and get them back because they've threatened not to pay us.' I jumped in my car and shot back to Mile End, but when I got there the inspector said that they had already gone to Stamford Hill, their main depot. When I told my manager this he said, 'In future always bring your tickets back here, you know what a ragtime outfit they are.'

Some of the drivers I knew often worked for Ewers (George Ewer was the owner of Grey-Green) and they told me to go to Stamford Hill if I could because they got all the good work. I phoned one weekend and they asked me where I lived, and they said, 'Stratford? Well go to Mile End and report there at seven o'clock.'

I got there and found it a bit strange. There were drivers coming in and doing their thing but nobody spoke to me, so I just hung about waiting. I did notice a driver come in and look at his day's work and then shout to the other drivers, 'Yarmouth service! They must be joking; I'm off home, see you.'

Their so-called inspector was told that the driver reported in sick so he called for me and said, 'Here, driver' and threw some papers at me: 'Yarmouth service.'

I looked at him and said, 'It's no use you giving that to me, I don't know your service stops and I am not sure of the way to Yarmouth,' and gave him back the paperwork. 'If it is not good enough for the regular driver then it's not good enough for me,' I thought. He went on to mumble something about bloody part-timers being a waste of space.

But another part-timer saw the Leyland Leopard standing there and said, 'I'll do it.'

'Good on you, mate,' I thought. Eventually the garage was cleared except for two coaches: a Leyland Leopard and a Bedford, and another spare driver who was off the buses. The inspector said, 'Do you think you can find your way over to Stamford Hill and take those two coaches? They will find you some work there.'

The bus driver asked if I would take the Leyland and then he would have the Bedford. We arrived at Stamford Hill and were given an afternoon tour to the Isle of Sheppey and Leysdown. I had to wait for him because he didn't know the way.

The Galleon manager phoned me on a Wednesday and asked if I could I help out on a three-day job to France.

'I've never been to France,' I said.

He told me there would be two drivers on two coaches. All I had to do was follow the other driver. So I thought, 'Why not?'

On the Friday morning I was given the oldest coach in the garage and the other regular driver had a brand-new Volvo. We had to pick up the passengers at Walthamstow swimming baths and take them to just outside Cherbourg.

One coach had to take the children and the other took the parents. I said to the other driver, 'You take the parents and I'll take the children.' But when the children came out and saw the new motor they were on it in a flash, so I had to have the parents.

We drove to Portsmouth and got the ferry to Cherbourg. We then drove about five miles inland to our hotels. The agenda for Saturday was that one coach had to take the children to the swimming baths in Cherbourg for practice and then an evening gala show and the other coach had to take the parents for a tour round while the children were busy in the morning.

I tried to get the other driver to do the tour but he insisted I had to do it. So I got my maps out and could see that if I ran along the coast to Barfleur and then to Carentan and back up on the N13 main road to Cherbourg and the hotel, I would have gone round in a triangle. I made a stop on the coastal road which the parents loved, saying that I must have done this before. I thought, 'Little do they know I haven't even been to France before, let alone driven there.' Of course, during my time on the coaches there was not as much continental work as there is now.

When I got back to the hotel, the other driver said, 'Where have you been? You were only supposed to take them for a little ride.'

That's what I'd done, I told him.

The children had their gala and when we reached home on the Sunday the parents all said how they had enjoyed the trip. As I had the parents as passengers I received more beer money than the other driver. However, we'd already said that we would share the spoils.

One of my friends said that there was a coach operator looking for part-timers in Purfleet, on the South Wales motorways. I thought, 'That sounds good, they must have some good motors.' I was wrong; they just had some clapped-out old Bedfords, but I gave it a try anyway.

One day I was given a commuter run to do from Hullbridge, in Essex, to Victoria Station, in London. I had to be at Hullbridge at seven o'clock so I was sitting there in the coach when the phone rang and the guv'nor asked where I was. I said, 'Sitting in the car park at Hullbridge, waiting.'

I was on hire to Stephensons coaches and apparently I had to drive past the guv'nor's house to get there and he had not seen me go by and wanted to know where I was. I said to my manager, 'Tell him not to blink otherwise he will miss me.'

What a day that was, waiting up in the city for the return journey at six o'clock and then on the trip down the coast the coach blew up and we all had to get another coach. I did not go back.

I did a bit for Swallows then, taking an old Ford coach to the coast where I met up with some Galleon coach drivers. 'What are you doing with that heap of rubbish?' they asked.

'I don't know. You tell me.'

I was once given a job on Galleon to take a party of people from Ilford to Watford. When I got to Ilford I found that it was a wedding party of a different nationality, I believe they were Indian. We were well on our way when one of the men asked if I could make a stop as I approached a roundabout. I thought that maybe they needed the toilet, but he said, 'No, I just want you to stop.' So I stopped just short of the roundabout and he got out and walked just a few paces away from the coach and smashed a coconut on the ground. He then got back in the coach and asked me to run over the milk.

I arrived at a Watford school and all the people went in except one man who sat in the coach talking to me. I said, 'Are you going in?'

He said, 'No, I am the Groom and I have to wait here until they call me in.'

He then went on to say that this was the third ceremony and tonight was the night it all happened. He mentioned that he would be staying at a hotel near where I lived, so I said I would come and see him and his wife and have a drink with them in the evening.

'No you bloody won't,' he exclaimed. 'I've waited long enough for this. I can do without visitors.' I had a good laugh at that.

He sat with me for some time and I said, 'They haven't forgotten you, have they?' but he assured me that they hadn't. Eventually someone came out to take him in and I was told there was food if I wanted any. I popped in for a bit while I was waiting; it looked like a temple, with a princess sitting on a throne and a big banquet of food on the tables. A man came out and said to me, 'Driver, if you have to turn the coach round, could you do it before the bride gets on the coach, because she must not go backwards.' So I turned the coach round and when all the passengers got on the man with the coconut smashed another on the ground, and asked me to drive over it. 'I hope I don't get a puncture driving over all these coconuts,' I said.

I arrived at Galleon one Sunday morning and noticed a Rolls Royce car there with dolly bird sitting inside it. I was told that it was a part-time driver's. We wondered why on earth he would want to do part-time coach driving if he was loaded.

We sat talking in the rest room, when suddenly there was an almighty crash. Everybody tried to get out the door together and when we finally looked we saw that the Rolls driver had reversed a coach down the pit. The manager was not pleased to see the sorry state the coach was in. He had a go at all the drivers, saying we should always get someone to watch us when a coach is on the pit.

The Rolls driver walked out, got in his car, went home and I never saw him again.

One weekend I was put on a job with my father and another driver. My father had been doing this party for a few years so he was in charge. We were taking a well-known wallpaper manufacturer's staff from East London to Margate for a firm's beano. My father allocated all the women to me and the pensioners to the other driver.

I watched all the beer going into my father's coach and then away we went. Our first stop was on death hill on the A20 (we always used the A20 when going to Margate, to cut out the Medway Towns and the traffic congestion). The women wanted to know why I had stopped with the men and I said, 'Well, they have got your beer.'

'No, that's the men's, so we want a pub,' they replied.

They all started arguing, so my father told me to take them to a pub just outside Margate and we would meet up there for the men's second session of drinks before lunch which we had booked for one o'clock at a hotel in Margate.

I started off and as I was going past a number of pubs the women started getting agitated and informed me that if I didn't stop at the next one we came to they were going to take my trousers off and rape me. Well, I didn't want telling twice as these were East End girls and I wouldn't put anything past them.

We stopped at this pub and they had a good old knees-up. However, they were all getting so drunk that I couldn't get them out to go to their one o'clock lunch appointment. Eventually I managed it and made a bold dash into Margate. I arrived an hour and a quarter late to find my father going spare. The girls came up to him and in my defence told him to 'f... off', and that he was not their driver, I was, and they took me to sit with them.

The men told my father to keep an eye on me on the way home because I had all their women and they did not want to lose them again at this pub. We rolled out of the pub at closing time but on the way home they wanted to stop for the toilets; I was told that I still had not escaped the chance of their raping me, so I should pull up at the next lay-by, which I did.

As it was in the dark, some managed to fall in a ditch and had their clothes and tights torn; when we got home they looked in a right mess. They all had a good time, though, and said that they looked forward to me taking them next year.

One weekend three coaches were to take a party of children to Colchester Zoo and I was selected as one of the drivers. We arrived at the zoo and after a meal we wandered around and eventually came to the rhino house. One of them was in a small shed-like enclosure, with not much room to turn, and as we stood watching it one of the drivers jumped over the stable gate and onto its back. We all fell about laughing at the crazy antics of this driver and thought what a nutter he was. This same driver was later sacked after he was caught with the wife of one of the passengers in his bedroom.

Some drivers always seemed to go a bit over the top when they were in a crowd; I think it was probably all bravado. My father once told me a story of when he went to Windsor with two other coaches. He and the other two drivers hired a boat on the river and were moving quite fast when one of the drivers said, 'Let's see if it goes as fast in reverse!' and pushed the gear lever into reverse so that the engine cut out with a grating noise from the gear box.

They could not restart the engine and had to be towed back to the boat hirer who was not best pleased. 'Why is it I always have trouble with you coach drivers?' he said.

I arrived at the coach garage one Friday morning to collect my wages and sat talking to the drivers in the mess room, when the office account lady came in to make tea and offered to make me one. I was then asked if I wanted a job on the Saturday to take a load of East End children to Southend, so I agreed.

There were four coaches on the job and on Saturday we picked up the children and went to Southend. I started talking to Bob, one of the drivers I had casually met before. He was going to take the coach and go to the bank, and I said that I didn't want to sit here all day so I would come for a ride with him.

We left Southend and I began to wonder where we were going when he pulled up outside a house in Stanford-le-Hope. 'This does not look like a bank,' I said, and he told me that this was where he lived. I was a bit shocked: 'If I knew you were coming home I would have stayed at Southend with the other drivers.'

'You didn't want to stay there all day did you?' he replied, introducing me to his wife who I immediately recognised from somewhere.

We kept trying to think where we had met to no avail,

when she suddenly said, 'I work in the coach garage three days a week and you are the tanker driver who I made a cup of tea for yesterday.'

From then on we became good friends and I eventually secured Bob an interview for a job at Gulf, which he got. It was in fact Bob who had taken his little boy for a ride and drowned him in gas oil that time.

Bob and I were called into the Galleon office and asked if we had passports and if not to get one, as they were starting to take holidaymakers to the south of Spain. They had got a contract from a well-known holiday company to run people down to the camp sites at Lloret de Mar and Blanes. We both got our passports but the regular drivers put a stop to part-time drivers doing these trips because they were a nice little earner, as it was a three-driver job on each coach.

Although the coaches were the modern Volvo B10s with a toilet and coffee-making facilities, they did not have a sleeping compartment for the drivers, so they had to try and sleep in the gangways, which was not good. When I met up with Ian once, I found out that somehow he had managed to do one, but he said that it was a killer of a drive so we were not missing much.

They would leave early Friday morning, pick up at Romford and go on their way, arriving in Spain on Saturday morning. They would drop off their passengers at the camp sites and then go round picking up all the returning holiday members, getting back home late Sunday evening. It was a non-stop trip.

Janne's sister and her husband would not fly and so decided to try a holiday abroad by coach. They went by a well-known coach operator who did camping holidays to Spain. One year they asked us if we would like to go as well and I thought 'Why not? I'll try anything once.' So we went and I got a little taste of what might have been. I was not impressed.

The coach driver's sleeping quarters were in what looked like a coffin and it occurred to me that if you were involved in an accident they would never find you. I thought 'no thanks' and kept one eye on the driver, because at times you noticed a little sway and I am sure it was them nodding off.

We had a married couple driving us and when we got to the toll booth she took the near-side mirror off, so they had no mirror and it was a right-hand drive coach. At the border of France and Spain they changed drivers and another young girl took over who would drive us to the camp sites, reload and then bring the coach back to the French border for the married couple to bring back home. In no uncertain terms she was not impressed with the missing mirror.

When the tachograph came into being (a device which records the speed and amount of time a driver has spent on the motor) in about 1983, I decided that I would have to give up part-time work on the coaches in case anything went wrong, especially with the hours I was driving. Maybe this development was a good thing, because on the beano trips, down to the coast, you were expected to be out until the sun shone the next morning and the passengers were drunk out of their skulls.

I was sorry to finish, but all good things have to come to an end. In 1999 I had a phone call from one of the younger drivers on Galleon who had been on the tankers with me and who was also a great friend, to say that Ian had died, my friend who had introduced me to Janne, who I owed everything to and who I had had many a good laugh and time with.

I phoned Vi and gave her my condolences. She said that they had tried every way to get in touch with me, but Gulf pensions would not give her my address or phone number, even though she told them that I would not want to miss his funeral. I will always remember the headlights and hazard lights flashing as we came together along the road. And his handshake.

Chapter 17

Leisure Time

WHILE I was at Gulf a number of the drivers bought caravans, so I bought one too and then a few of us could go away for weekends. I got on with one driver named Jim and his family in particular as he had two daughters the same age as ours. He also had a son named Jamie who was about four years old; Jamie and I became mates, wherever I went he would follow me. Jamie was a lovely looking boy, with blond hair down to his neck with a fringe and he was motor mad. Maybe we got on because he reminded me of myself at his age; the only difference was that my father didn't have a car like his did.

My caravan had a double bed at one end and a bunk bed at the other end and I was a bit concerned about the top bunk in case one of the girls fell out. Eventually, when we were holidaying in Wales, Angela did fall out, so the next day I went and found a hardware shop and bought some wood and rope to tie her in. I later bought a new van with a double bed at each end as the children were getting bigger by then, so I did not have to worry about them falling out.

We went to Newquay for our holidays one year and while we were parked up at the caravan site a man came over to tell us that Jamie had left the lights on in Jim's car. We both had estate cars so we took turns in using them on day trips as you could get two children in the back. We went to start Jim's car, but Jamie had flattened the battery. However, Jim was still insisting we took his car. It would not start, so we jump-started it and I said, 'Let's take the spare battery with us.'

But Jim said, 'No, after a short run the alternator will have charged it enough.'

We went and parked at the National Trust car park at Hollywell Bay on the downs and walked down to the beach and spent all day there. In the late afternoon we returned to the car but it would not start. I said, 'We should have brought the spare battery,' but Jim started taking the points and plugs out and cleaning them. 'Doing that is not going to make the slightest difference,' I said, but we all lay out on the grass sunbathing while he stripped the engine.

In the end he had to agree there was nothing we could do and as we were the only ones left in the car park we had to go and find someone to give us a start. We sent Janne and Jim's wife Maureen to a nearby farm for help. While crossing the fields they encountered some horses and ran for their lives, but they managed to get through and to persuade a farmer to come out with a beat-up old car and jump-start us.

I remember once going into a bank with Jim and leaving the car parked on a slope with the wives and children in it. While we were in the bank Jamie apparently got behind the steering wheel and we came out to find the car on the other side of the car park and the girls and wives shouting at Jamie. My car was a Vauxhall estate so the handbrake was on the right under the dash and as he had got in he had grabbed the handbrake to help him in and had accidentally released it. A man had got in and stopped it before any damage was done. Maureen said, 'I don't know what he bloody done, but we started going backwards.'

The caravan did not ride well, even though I had anti-jackknife equipment fitted, loaded it properly and checked the nose weight, it just was not right. So when my mate Jamie rode with us he used to sit in the back seat with the girls on the off-side looking out the window to the rear for lorries. He would shout, 'Here comes one, Al! Come on you git. Hold tight, Al, she's swaying, she's swaying!' The first time we heard him I couldn't stop laughing.

Once when we were leaving to come home we decided to travel through the night. We said, 'We'll find a pub and have a drink before it gets too late.'

We found a pub and pulled in the car park alongside each other and Jim and I went into the pub to get the drinks while the girls stayed with the vans. We sat down in Jim's caravan chatting and enjoying our drinks when Jim said, 'Where's Jamie?'

We found him walking round the cars and as it was getting dark Jim put the lights on in the van. After some time the lights went dim and we looked at each other trying to figure out what it was and then the caravan started moving and jumping. All of a sudden the penny dropped and we all tried getting out of the van together.

We eventually got out and Jamie was standing over the other side of the car park shouting, 'It's all right, Dad! I switched it off!'

It turned out that Jamie had switched on the ignition to play the radio but had turned too far. The car had been left in gear and the engine had been about to start with us all in the caravan.

Once, when we were camping in Suffolk, Jamie wanted to take our spaniel for a walk round the camp site. I decided to go to the loo and met Jamie coming back with the dog and he was covered in mud and soaking wet. I asked him what happened and he said he fell in the pond. So I said, 'Janne will go mad when she sees you.' He maintained that he fell, but we think he was pushed; that's Jamie.

He used to come and see me when it was getting dark to go moonlighting (as he called it). We would take our torches and shine them up in the trees and look for birds, the feathery kind of course.

He was a great little dancer and would always be on the dance floor. Suddenly he would jump down, do the splits, and jump up just as quick and people standing watching the dancers would say, 'Did you see that little boy do the splits?'

Whenever Jim and I were on a run together at Gulf Jamie would ride with me and I would say to him, 'Let's get on the freeway and burn some rubber.' I joked all the time with him and I think he enjoyed me sodding about.

We were once on nights delivering to a depot in Bedfordshire on a frosty winter's night when Jim had a hydraulic leak and some gas oil had spilt on the ground. When Jim and I had finished pumping off I had to run through the oil and then we had a short distance to travel along a country lane until we approached the main road which was down a slight incline.

As I started to brake, the Leyland Marathon, a vehicle I had no confidence in, started sliding on the frosty and oil-soaked tyres, so I had to check the skid and hope it did not jack-knife. I managed to stop, but I looked across at Jamie and saw that he was terrified. I don't know what I looked like, but it was a fright to say the least. He said, 'Can I go with my Dad?' and it was then I thought that, although I liked him riding with me, if anything happened to him, I could not forgive myself.

I flashed Jim up and he stopped in a lay-by so I pulled in behind him. Jamie looked across to me and said, 'I've changed my mind, I'm going to stay with you, because he is a bloody sight madder than you are.'

Of course today Jamie is a married man and has his own family. But I'll never forget him and the excitement he brought to our camping holidays. You never knew what would happen next.

Chapter 18

Retirement

I am now in my retirement. I'm not a lot of good in the garden, as Janne would tell you, though I do a bit of DIY when the call comes. We have been abroad quite a few times, especially as Janne's sister's husband was going blind, so he wanted to go to Spain by coach quite often. We did this a couple of times and sometimes we went away with both my daughters, my son-in-law and my grandson, which was nice.

I still wanted a part-time job, however, so when I saw an advertisement for drivers at Purfleet Deep Wharf, taking new cars off the Ro-Ro (roll-on/roll-off) car ferries and reloading it, I applied and got the job. This was in 2004, when I was seventy-two years old.

I had a choice of starting times; I could start from six in the morning, two in the afternoon, ten in the evening, or do nights. I chose the early mornings as I wanted to get home and have the afternoon free. This job was the dock staff's really, but with so many trailers coming in and out they had to pass the work to outside labour. This did not go down well with some of the dock staff and they showed this in various ways.

For example, to use the toilets we had to go out of the building and walk round the outside and come in at the far end, as we were not allowed through their mess room.

After they had done their shift on the trailers with a tug unit, as they called them, they would then come and work with us, but it was always 'them and us' and they didn't often talk to you; I felt like an outcast.

We had all sorts of new cars to get off the ferries, from Mercs, to Minis and Smart cars. We would then reload with the exports such as Land Rovers, vans, farm tractors and sometimes lorries.

I spoke to one of the men working the tugs and he asked me what I did for my living and I told him I was on tankers. He said, 'Why don't you come on the tugs?' 'I am a bit too old for that now,' I thought.

I stayed for about three months but I could not get on with the dock staff and their ways, so I packed it up.

A few months later I met up with a driver I had been on Aero with, who was the same age as me. We started chatting and he said, 'I've got a job for you, if you want it.' I said that I did and he said, 'The Japanese import auctions in Tilbury Docks want drivers to take the cars through the auction rooms.'

'It's not a six o'clock start is it?' I asked.

'No, we start at nine o'clock and do some tidying up in the yard and then at eleven o'clock the cars are driven through the shed and sold off. Then we park them up and come home at three in the afternoon; it is £6 an hour.'

So I started. There were ten drivers, mostly pensioners, and we had a good laugh. After about three months the auction said they were packing up and we were all disappointed because it had only been one day a week and it suited all of us as it was a doddle.

I decided to buy a camper van that year so that we could go away at weekends and maybe to Scotland for a holiday.

So we tried it out a couple of times and then decided to go for two weeks to Scotland with Lee-Anne.

When I got to Braemar I kept asking people, 'What have you done with the Devil's Elbow?' Everyone from the younger generation I spoke to looked at me in bewilderment and thought I was a bit barmy, but eventually I found a tourist board office and asked two older ladies what had happened to it, as I had come up a nice new wide road.

They replied, 'You can still see it if you look over to the right as you come along the road,' and then produced a book full of pictures of coaches negotiating the 'S' bend. So I told them that I used to drive up it with a coach.

Another thing I remember is stopping at the Royal Hotel in Tyndrum, a hotel on its own on the moors, with the big log fires that were always blazing when we arrived. We got to Tyndrum, which was a small village, and I said to Lee-Anne who was driving, 'Carry on for a few miles, because I want to see the hotel.' We travelled for some time and then I said, 'They must have pulled it down, let's turn back and stop at one of the cafés in Tyndrum.' I noticed another tourist board office and so I went over to them and asked where the Royal Hotel was. He looked at me and said that it was behind the café. I walked round the back of the café and there was the hotel. When I used to come here it was right by the road side, but it looks like they have bought the road out so that the hotel now lies further back.

Even the Isle of Skye, which had had a ferry to take us across to the island, where the ferrymen always offered the coach drivers a wee dram, and where you could not get off the island on a Sunday as everything came to a standstill, now has a bridge going over to it.

We tried to get to Balloch one day, where we used to put the passengers on the boats for trips on Loch Lomond, but somehow we bypassed it because of the new roads that had been put in. Also, I could not believe how built up Gretna Green had become, with a housing estate and such like. Well, I suppose it was forty-odd years ago that I came. Scotland is just not how I remembered it; it is now too commercialised everywhere. I would rather have seen it how I remembered it.

I am seventy-six now and often think back to my touring days. I have driven all over England, Scotland and Wales and wouldn't even try to guess the number of miles I've covered.

I've driven in torrential rain, been brought to a standstill by snowdrifts, have experienced such dense fog that I needed someone to walk in front of the coach with a lighted torch to guide me in.

Other Books and DVDs from Old Pond Publishing

Scania at Work PATRICK W DYER
This highly illustrated book shows how Scania developed from the L75. This is a book for an enthusiast, by an enthusiast. Hardback book.

Tuckers North Truckers South LESLIE PURDON
In 1945, Shay leaves school to become a trailer-boy on an Atkinson truck and is taught to love life on the road by the driver, who knows all the tricks of the trade. Paperback book.

Juggernaut Drivers LESLIE PURDON
A light-hearted read for everyone who likes trucks and trucking, featuring a fictional gang of 1970s owner-operators. In good times they run legal; in bad times they cut corners. Paperback book.

Ice Road Truckers
Series One and Two of this spell-binding documentary by the History Channel follow the truckers as they endure one of the most perilous stretches of road in the world. Each series includes 3 discs. DVD.

Hell Drivers
Ex-con Tom (Stanley Baker) has no option but to haul ballast for Hawletts in this 1950s feature film. 'Twelve runs a day or you're sacked', is the threat that hangs over the drivers as they speed their Dodge trucks along narrow lanes. DVD.

Destination Doha
In this 1977 BBC programme meet the extraordinary men who form the 5,000 mile transport link between Britain and the Arabian Gulf. Parts One and Two are both included in this two-disc set. DVD.

Free complete catalogue:

Old Pond Publishing Ltd, Dencora Business Centre, 36 White House Road, Ipswich IP1 5LT, United Kingdom

Secure online ordering: **www.oldpond.com**

Phone: 01473 238200